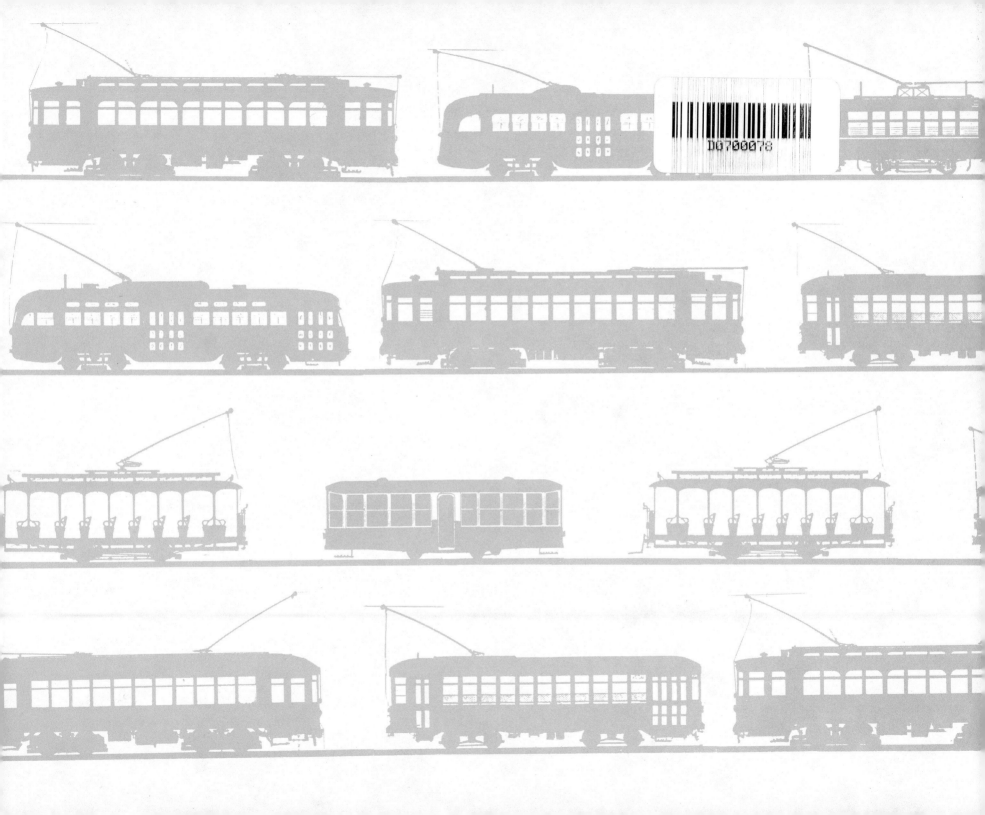

The COLORFUL STREETCARS We Rode

Bulletin 125
Central Electric Railfans' Association

The COLORFUL STREETCARS We Rode

Central Electric Railfans' Association

Bulletin 125

The COLORFUL STREETCARS We Rode

Bulletin 125 of the Central Electric Railfans' Association

Copyright © 1986 by the Central Electric Railfans' Association
All rights reserved
An Illinois Not-for-Profit Corporation
Post Office Box 503, Chicago, Illinois 60690, U.S.A.

Library of Congress Catalog Card Number 85-081490
International Standard Book Number 0-915348-25-x

EDITORIAL STAFF
    Norman Carlson
    William C. Janssen
    George Krambles
    Arthur H. Peterson
AUTHOR, SPECIAL TEXTS
    Jury Leonid Koffman

CERA Bulletins are technical, educational references prepared as historical projects by members of the Central Electric Railfans' Association, working without salary due to their interest in the subject. This Bulletin is consistent with this stated purpose of the corporation: To foster the study of the history, equipment and operation of electric railways. If you can provide additional information, or are of the opinion that any statement herein is inaccurate or incomplete, please send documentation supporting such amendment or correction, citing sources, to the Central Electric Railfans' Association, P.O. Box 503, Chicago, Illinois 60690, U.S.A.

The COLORFUL STREETCARS We Rode was designed by George Krambles. Color separations and assembly are by Jim Walter Graphic Arts of Beloit, Wisconsin with typesetting by Guetschow Typesetting of South Beloit, Illinois. This book was printed by Sorg Printing Company of Illinois and bound by Zonne Bookbinders of Chicago, Illinois.

ACKNOWLEDGMENTS

There is a certain magic to an all-color book. Mention the concept—the support and enthusiasm follow immediately. There was no difficulty at all in getting people to contribute the rarest photographic gems in their collections. In fact, the challenge was to get all of the available information into a compact format.

CERA "project foreman" for Bulletin 125 was George Krambles. George worked virtually full time for four months to complete this book, pushing into overtime to carry on his normal work of transit consulting. Not only did he research the captions, but he did the layout and all the word processing. George's vast knowledge of the transit industry was very valuable in this work. He also created most of the pen and ink sketches.

Pleased as we are that George Krambles has returned as an active member of CERA's publication staff after an absence of many, many years, we are equally delighted to introduce the work of Jury Leonid Koffman, author of the several interesting texts which complement the photographs. They add another kind of color to this very colorful volume.

Mr. Koffman brings a lifetime of experience in the railway and transit field to this book. A new threshold for CERA publication staff, in addition to our home office in Chicago, has now been opened in Leicester, England, where Jury resides. But with telephone communication by satellite and overnight airmail, coordination has proved quite manageable. Jury's enthusiasm for *The COLORFUL CARS We Rode* was contagious. His scholarly approach caused us to turn over many new and old stones to research more information. So that you may become aware of a little of Jury's contributions to transportation engineering in several countries, we have taken the unusual step of including a brief biography of him. Don't miss it!

Of course, many others have provided immeasurably through their support in supplying pictures, helping ferret out others, untangling incomplete or tangled references and in countless other ways. Among these, we especially thank the following, "for service beyond the call . . . "

Richard F. Begley	Roy G. Benedict	Bill Billings	Howard R. Blackburn
Eugene R. Boswell	Charles A. Brown	James J. Buckley	Frank E. Butts
Joseph N. Canfield	Norton D. Clark	O. R. Cummings	R. L. Day
Raymond DeGroote	Harre W. Demoro	Arthur D. Dubin	Donald Duke
George W. Gerhart	Robert C. Gerstley	Francis J. Goldsmith	Donald William Harold
Paul Herz, Jr.	Charles V. Hess	J. Wallace Higgins	Lawson K. Hill
William C. Janssen	Seymour Kashin	Ralph Kerchum	Albert D. Kerr
LeRoy O. King, Jr.	Peter Kocan	Thomas A. Lesh	Gordon E. Lloyd
Morris H. Lloyd	Richard N. Lukin	Willis A. McCaleb	George G. McKinley
Robert V. Mehlenbeck	William D. Middleton	William F. Nedden	Arthur H. Peterson
Elaine L. Peterson	Jerry D. Pruden	John A. Rehor	Edward Ridolph
William E. Robertson	Anthony J. Schill	Fred W. Schneider III	William H. Schriber
James P. Shuman	Robert Smith	Charles A. Smallwood	Henry Stange
Art Stitzel	Allen Styffe	Eugene Van Dusen	George H. Yater

and posthumously:

Arthur R. Alter	Howard S. Babcock	Frank M. Brown	Thomas H. Desnoyers

It is our objective that each CERA publication strive to advance the state of the art and set the example for those to follow. Two friends of CERA had a significant role in this book. Jim Walter took unusual care in creating the color separations to achieve maximum reproduction quality as well as arranging for many production details. Wally Maier of Sorg Printing contributed ideas to improve the printing of this book. This book could only be accomplished by the collective effort of all of those mentioned. To them, and to you readers who continue to support CERA we say, "Thank you very much!"

Norman Carlson
for the CERA publications team

Chicago, November 1985

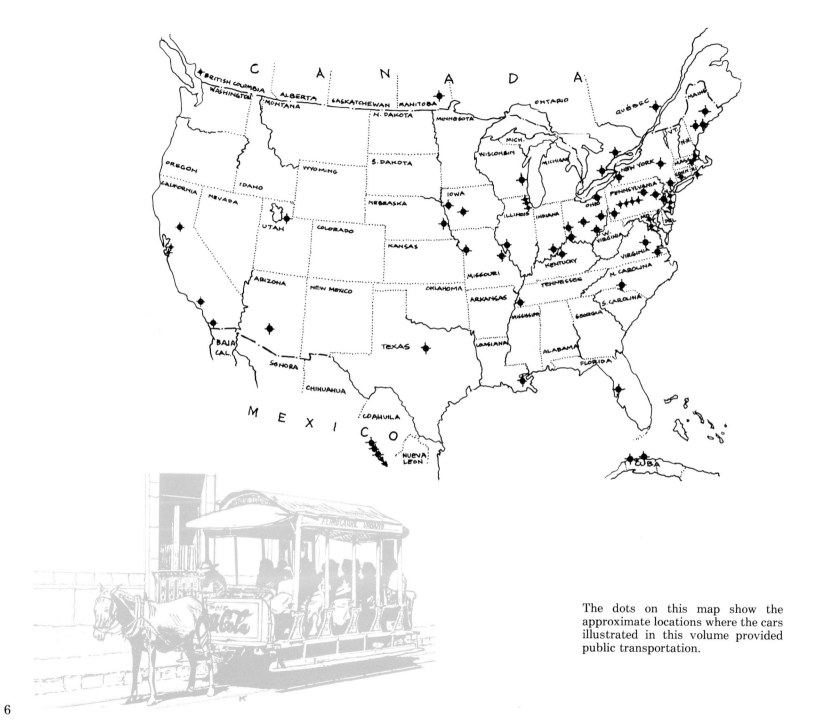

The dots on this map show the approximate locations where the cars illustrated in this volume provided public transportation.

The COLORFUL STREETCARS We Rode

REMEMBER WHEN Trolley Wires Spanned the Country, Bulletin 119 of the Central Electric Railfans' Association (1980), commemorated over forty years of CERA by revisiting in photographs many North American electric railway operations of that period. The narrative captions emphasized historical aspects of the subjects.

Encouraging reader response has mandated that we present as CERA Bulletin 125 an entirely new selection of illustrations within the same time and territorial span of coverage, that is, 1939-1964 in the United States, Canada, Mexico and Cuba. In this second study many cities and systems not included in *REMEMBER WHEN* are represented, a truly remarkable fact when one considers that color film was new, costly and scarce until after World War II. Cameras to handle 35mm film cost much more than they do today measured in current dollars in each case! But one of the great rewards yielded by the publication of *REMEMBER WHEN* is that it triggered many new contributors to share their most prized photographs in this volume.

The coverage of this book ends in the mid 1960s, in some ways a nadir in the history of electric railways. For it was about that time when public policy first began to recognize that transit did indeed have a permanent place in supporting the urban economy through the foreseeable future. Reserved for future books are new starts and new cars that came into existence after the mid 1960s. This would include of course: Atlanta, Baltimore, Buffalo, Calgary, Detroit, Edmonton, Lowell, Miami, Portland, Sacramento, San Diego, San Jose, Toronto, Vancouver plus others from among the many now in planning that come to life in the meantime. In CERA Bulletin 119 we said, "Not since the early days of the century has the future of the industry looked brighter." The passage of five more years has reaffirmed that prediction.

Almost all of the photographs in this volume are being published for the first time. The narrative text and captions have been especially developed to emphasize the development of the rolling stock and to recognize some of the people who contributed over time to the art and science represented in street railway technology. Included as sidebars are essays featuring some milestone achievements in streetcar design and their creators.

As one pages through this book, the variety among streetcars becomes obvious. Today, when mass production of standardized hardware has its own cult of devotees, it is worth noting that variety and gradual evolution (as in nature itself) also has merit in perfecting the process and its hardware. Join the photographers and authors in remembering the fascinating world of street railways which members of the Central Electric Railfans' Association were privileged to witness during CERA's first quarter century.

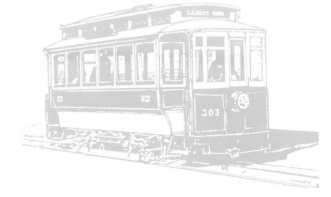

F C Urbano De Celaya

Before the advent of electric traction, a horse (or in this case, a mule) was often the motive power for moving people by streetcar. Horsecars were designed to be as light in weight as possible. To hold weight down to what one animal ▲ could reasonably pull, overall length was limited, typically to about 16 ft. Many open horsecars were hardly more than a flat deck with benches covered with a light roof supported by thin posts.

Unbelievably, in 1953 this bit of antiquity was still serving Celaya, Mexico.

Photo: J. Wallace Higgins

British Columbia Electric Railway 123

In Montreal, observation trolleys were introduced in 1905 and continued their rounds on nice summer days until 1958. Cars of similar design, incorporating a theater-like cascade of seats, were operated in Canada in Quebec City, ▶▲ Calgary and Vancouver, whose car 123 is shown here in 1950. The inspiration for using sightseeing cars on a street railway is said to have come from the Louisana Purchase Exposition in St. Louis in 1904, a fair that was quite a showplace for the new street car technology of that day.

Photo: Richard R. Andrews

San Francisco Municipal Railway 367

The need to operate on grades of up to 14% and around sharp curves of San Francisco's Union Street line led Paul J. Ost and M. M. O'Shaugnessy to develop this unusual car for the Municipal Railway about 1921. A sample was ▶▶ built by A. Meister & Sons Company of Sacramento; 20 more were outshopped in 1922 by American Car Company of St. Louis.

The 29 ft. sample car, #200, which cost $15,000, seated 32, and could handle 55-60 people. The body was semi-steel and rode on a Brill "Radiax" (radial axle) truck. It was powered with two Westinghouse 532-A, 50 hp. 600 v motors, geared 15:57. K-36 control was supplied by General Electric, together with a line breaker, as a precaution against alarming passengers should the breaker open while climbing a steep hill. There were air-operated tread brakes for normal service plus manually operated track brakes for emergency. Photo of car 367 taken 1947; car scrapped 1948.

Photo: A. R. Alter, from Bill Billings collection

8

Biddeford & Saco Railroad 246

This was a trolley line of about eight miles extending between the two towns of its name in Maine, passing en route the better known resort of Old Orchard Beach. Its life (1892-1939) saw little change in the pleasant rural area it traversed other than the critical shift to private autos on good hard roads.

It listed 31 cars, of which #246 was typical. Built in 1911 for the Portland (Maine) Railroad, it was recorded in this 1938 photo at Biddeford.

Photo: Charles A. Brown

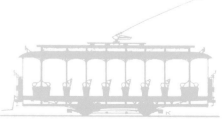

10

OPEN STREET CARS IN THE U.S.A.

Originally prepared for *Strassenbahn Magazin*
Edited by CERA for presentation in English

The rapid spread of electric street railways in the United States following Frank J. Sprague's inventions demonstrated by the 1888 opening of the lines in Richmond, Virginia, led to the wide spread use of open cars. Such cars were most common along the east coast, not only for the usual summer traffic, but also because of their considerable popularity for excursion and party services and even for accommodating church groups.

To foster weekend riding, many operators built amusement parks adjoining lakes or the sea coast, usually well outside city limits to be sure to generate some trolley fares. Lima Park at Coney Island was an example. These so-called "Electric Parks," of which there were no less than 467 by the year 1907, provided open air and closed theaters, restaurants, bathing areas and numerous other amusement facilities. They were definitely important traffic generators for the traction companies.

The then-weekly *Street Railway Journal*, later *Electric Railway Journal* (abandoned 1942), devoted whole issues in 1907 and 1908 to street railway amusement parks, analyzing their offerings critically.

They reported that some parks had been located close to carbarns so that the night shift could do necessary park maintenance including changing the records on the automatic player pianos! In an extreme example, the Waterville Fairfield & Oakland Street Railway (Maine) built an integrated facility at Messalonskee Lake that had a restaurant and boat house on the lake bank, a three-track carbarn above these and another restaurant and dance floor on the roof.

Among establishments of this type, Wildwood Park of the Twin Cities Rapid Transit Company (Minneapolis-St. Paul, Minnesota) was outstanding. It was located on White Bear Lake and reached by street railway along the "Route of Greenery and Scenery." Visitors could enjoy the beauty of the countryside and various hotels offered meals, refreshments and accommodations. On the opposite end of the system, Minnetonka Lake invited steamer excursions (in boats built and operated by TCRT) on routes extending over 20 miles.

Elsewhere use was made of more unusual possibilities for traffic promotion. Thus the Pacific Electric Railway encouraged the local national guard to hold a public exercise by providing ammunition in addition to free rides, to a place not usually much frequented by visitors but handy to the railway. About 10,000 spectators responded, one car arriving with 160 passengers, 43 of them riding on the roof!

During 1907 some fifty million passengers were encouraged to visit these establishments and open cars served most of them. But open cars were popular for ordinary journeys on hot summer days, too, at a time when radio, television and the movies, not to speak of air conditioning, were all in the future.

The exhilaration of motion and fresh air coming from all sides induced a feeling of physical and mental well-being not attainable in horse-drawn carriages. About 1900, a well-known physician in Louisville, Kentucky stated that, on the basis of careful investigations he found that the ride in an open streetcar was a very good way to avoid insomnia. He suggested that before going to bed one should go for a one or two hour ride on an open car, preferable on the front seat! The feeling of tiredness would almost always set in and a good night's sleep would be the pleasant reward! He did not report what effect the experience may have had on the motormen and conductors who worked open cars all evening. . . .

Smoking in those days was considered to be at least an unpleasant vice and smokers were as much as possible encouraged to use the open cars, preferably on the rear seats. As *Street Railway Journal* reported:

Oh, what delight
   On a soft June night
To ride in an open car.
   You can stand the expense,
It's only five cents,
   No matter how poor you are.

In the three rear pews
   You may smoke if you choose,
'Tis the rule of the open car.
   But you'll hear, I'm afraid,
Some funny old maid
   Say, "Oh, that horrid seegar!"

The cars were fitted with from seven to fifteen throwover benches. Each could seat five or six people, so that 35 to 90 seats were available on a car. Sometimes, as for example in Boston, the capacity was increased still further to get 110 seated passengers aboard one car.

Car weights varied between six and fourteen tons without passengers. Power was occasionally provided by only one motor, but more typically by two or four motors of 25 or 30 hp each. A few big cars had two 60 hp motors.

Overall car length varied between 35' and 46' and the seat (and roof pillar) spacing was typically around 30'. Overall car width varied between 84" and 90", with a few cars up to 98", not including steps, which brought width out an additional 12".

Floor height varied between 33" and 36" above rail, with the first step typically at the 18" to 21" level. Truck wheelbase for single-truckers was as little as 78". Double-truckers had 48" to 63" wheelbase trucks, with the truck centers at about 14'-3". For satisfactory operation, wheelbase should be about 0.2 x track curve radius, coming to 70". (Failing to meet this limit may be one reason it's not possible to run the Berlin center-entrance car, having a 10'-8" wheelbase, over the Seashore Museum line at Kennebunkport, Maine).

The axle-hung motor with double-reduction gear as evolved by Sprague was the classic propulsion package and it was copied by Sprague's greatest competitor, the Thomson-Houston company, which soon overtook him. Their motor incorporated a simpler and more robust layout, with carbon brushes and multi-notch resistor control. This motor, known as the F 30 (signifying two 15 hp motors per car) was supplied in the amazing quantity of 4,621. It was followed by the WP 50, standing for waterproof 2 x 25 hp. This had a split housing enclosing the armature and the field winding, there being only one field coil for the upper pole, the coil for the lower pole being eliminated to avoid problems with moisture. No less than 7,638 of this model were produced.

Consolidation of Thomson-Houston with Edison General Electric to form the General Electric Company was followed by introduction of the GE-800 motor, developing 25 hp. The "800" indicated the tractive effort of 800 lb. delivered at the rim of 33" wheels if driven by this machine.

As far as controllers were concerned, a significant step also made by General Electric at the beginning of the 1890s was the development of the K-type series-parallel controllers which became standard over several decades. The design was conceived by Porter and Parshall, the latter having been involved with the original equipment of the Central London Underground, whose chairman he ultimately became.

The K controller incorporated a magnetic blow-out as developed by Professor Thomson to deal with arcs that otherwise occurred during notching. K-type controllers had no braking notches. Open cars were usually fitted with the K-6 type having six series and five parallel notches; the K-10 (5s + 4p), the K-28 (5s + 5p) or the K-35 (5s + 3p).

Although open cars were seasonally very popular with riders and were acquired in large quantity (there were more than 25,000 in service at their peak), they were not so highly valued by the owners. The ability of passengers to board and alight along the entire car length was helpful in reducing time at stops, but on the other hand, the cross-benches made the work of conductors more difficult for they had to collect fares by moving along the narrow step, clinging on with one hand at all times. Where inspectors were used to check tickets, their work was equally difficult and hazardous. Fraud was rampant in fare collection.

In the older town centers where narrow streets precluded more than single track, cars moved very slowly and passengers were constantly boarding and alighting from moving cars. While most male passengers seemed able to get on or off fairly easily by facing forward, the ladies for some unknown reason, tended to jump off with their back toward the car front, often with disastrous results. Many people seemed to consider it their right to board or alight from either side of cars (as one can observe today on San Francisco's cable cars), all too often directly into the path of opposing traffic. Some companies covered the left side of their cars with screens to prevent this, but that meant climbing over several people to get to a vacant left side seat. Others, wanting to control access, rearranged their cars with a center aisle, wire covered both sides and handled boarding and alighting from the vestibules as with closed cars.

It is interesting to note how women's styles have affected car design. Around 1910 it became fashionable to wear skirts quite long and close fitting. Ladies learned to take short, mincing steps rather than long strides which were impossible in such skirts unless one lifted the skirt. That could be done with a saucy flare, revealing a bit of ankle and calf, considered at the time to be quite provocative to the men. In some puritanical communities such a revelation was considered morally corrupting; ordinances forbad it and made it a police responsibility to enforce modesty! Open cars, with their steep side steps, became a likely place to find offenders.

There were other valid safety reasons for keeping step riser height within limits. During 1913-1914 regulatory bodies in a number of states ruled that no step was to exceed 17″. In the meantime, J. G. Brill Company, back in 1905, created its "Narragansett" design, which provided a shorter top riser by recessing a step into the side sill/floor structure of open cars.

Since the roof of an open car was carried by relatively slim posts, the whole superstructure was not very stiff when it came to collision strength, and there were occasions when the roof would collapse on the passengers. A case in point took place in Philadelphia on the evening of May 24, 1908. Five open cars were climbing a hill. Behind them at the bottom of the hill a closed car was standing. The 50-seat open cars were carrying 70-85 passengers except for the lead car which had 100. The 32-seat closed car had 90 riders. The lead car's circuit breaker tripped on overload and was reclosed by the motorman only to blow the main fuse. The car began drifting backwards down the hill, hitting the other four open cars in succession, the whole finally coming to a stop by plowing into the standing closed car!

The company blamed the motorman but he claimed that the handbrake staff broke off and subsequently that a passenger at the rear tried to actuate the brake making further braking impossible. The blame was later shifted to "pickpockets who pulled the trolley from the wire to facilitate their working in the dark." Whatever the reason, four of the open cars were levelled to the floor and had to be written off, four passengers were killed and 250 injured, 63-75 sufficiently to require hospitalization!

The main disadvantage of open cars was that they could really only be used in warm, dry weather. Opaque canvas duck curtains could be lowered during a rain storm, but they made boarding and alighting a puzzling chore.

For colder periods a second fleet of cars with closed bodies were needed and this meant higher investment, maintenance and stabling costs. Some companies sought to cut these costs by having only one set of trucks, motors and control and swapping these seasonally between open and closed bodies, with the out-of-season shells stored. Others took less drastic measures such as removing only two of the four motors from closed cars and putting them into the lighter summer cars, or removing summer car motors and control seasonally to power snowplows. Unfortunately, all such measures burdened the companies with recurrent costs and tied up shop manpower needed for maintenance work. Carbodies stored without motors were vulnerable to carbarn fires, an all-too-frequent occurrence then.

For a time there was a variant of the open car that was very popular in the western United States, the "California" car, which had a body that was divided longitudinally into an open section and a closed one. This could be said to allow the rider to vote where to ride, but in practice it usually meant overcrowding of one section or the other according to the prevailing weather. This type of car continues in service today on San Francisco's cable cars.

A kind of last straw in the life of the open car was the difficulty of converting one for operation with one-person crew. For this reason, a number of summer cars were rebuilt to closed bodies after 1920 while many were scrapped. By the early 1930s only a few remained, notably at the Five-Mile Beach Railway (New Jersey), the Fairmount Park line in Philadelphia, and (for football traffic) on the Connecticut Company at New Haven.

J. L. K.

Brill 39-E-1
Maximum Traction Truck

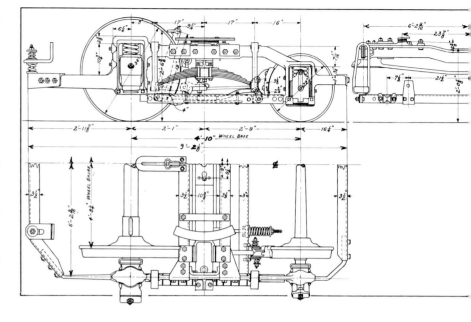

JOHN A. BRILL'S MAXIMUM TRACTION TRUCK

Around the turn of the century there was rapid spread of cities facilitated by the development and speed of electric railways. The resulting growth of local traffic made the introduction of operationally attractive, high-capacity cars a necessity. Four-wheelers could no longer ensure either an attractive or economic solution to the problems faced by many operators. Their popularity was rapidly dropping to an all-time low just at the time franchises needed to be renewed, and favorable relations with political authorities were imperative. Operating costs of single-truck cars were burdened by the need to have a conductor on *every* car, motor or trailer alike. Although there already were many double-truck cars, existing technology left them with poor ride qualities, together with other engineering and operational problems, both electrical and mechanical.

Prevailing motor dimensions and snow clearance requirements demanded the use of 30″-33″ diameter wheels. These were accommodated beneath the floor of a single-truck design without resulting in a floor height too great for good passenger circulation. Control for two-motor equipment was state-of-the-art. Four-motor control was not. Purely on the basis of construction and operation, double-truck vehicles would not cause undue difficulty were it not for having to negotiate curves of as little as 30′ radius in city streets. A brief technical analysis illustrates:

The throwover x of a truck depends on the distance between truck centers L, the curve radius R, and the longitudinal distance between the point concerned and the kingpin, l, thus: $x = L\, l\, / \, 2\, R$
$= 16″$ when $R = 30′$, $L = 20′$, and $l = 4′$
Alternatively, with an outside hung motor, the truck wheelbase could be reduced to 4′-6″, in which case x would be reduced to about 12″, but this would tend to result in a more lively ride, both on tangent and curved track.

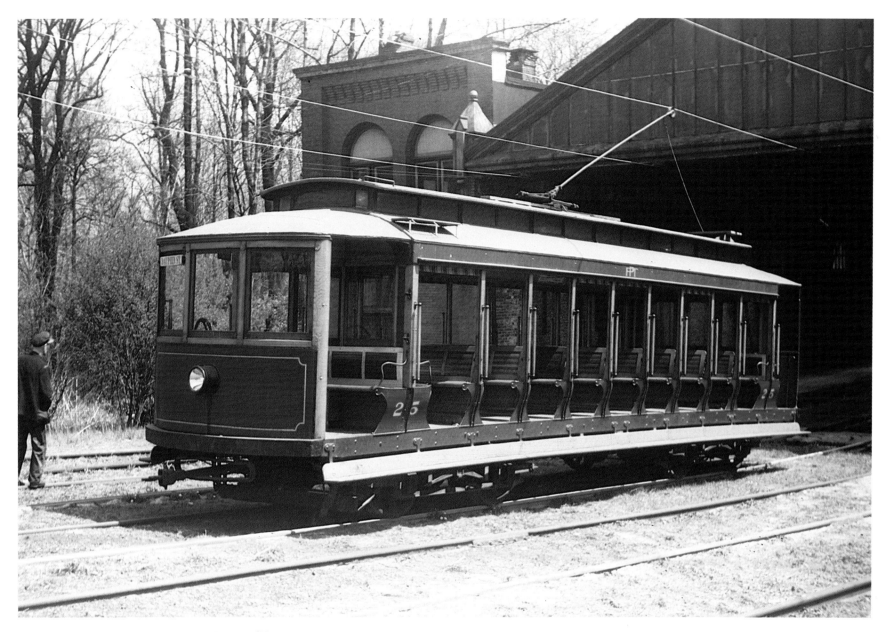

Fairmount Park Transit 25

Operating (from 1896) some 15 miles of 62½" gage track entirely within a central city park made the Fairmount Park Transit unique. Its fleet of 55 cars (26 of them trailers) included both open summer cars and closed ones. The open cars originally had unenclosed platforms. Glazing was added for the comfort of the motorman and other folks up front.

Photo: Charles A. Brown

To accommodate prevailing body and truck construction, floor height either had to be raised or the side sills spread sufficiently to allow the truck to swing freely when running through curves. This usually meant two steps would be needed and car weight would increase. With the then-current preference for two motors (either one in each truck or two in one truck and none in the other), hill climbing ability was restricted, a rather important fault to some operators and their real estate associates. Increased weight concentration of double-truck cars proved an embarrassment to some track, which, to quote traction pioneer Frank J. Sprague, was on occasion built "for profit and not for permanence."

To meet this challenge, a highly attractive solution was proposed by John Albert Brill (1852-1908), the engineering brain of Philadelphia-based J.G. Brill Company, founded by his father in 1868. Brill's idea was the "Eureka Maximum Traction Truck." As it happens, "Maximum Traction" was not an exact description for a load distribution giving more than 50% load on driving wheels, since this could not ensure the *highest* possible tractive force. Genuine maximum traction on a double-truck car would have a motor on each of the four axles. However, the flattering name stuck and the design quickly became widely adopted by street railways around the world.

The driving wheelset, with inside-hung motor, was provided in the U.S. with 30"-33" wheels (31½" in Germany, 26"-30" in England). The pony (un-motored) wheelsets had 20"-22" diameter wheels. The truck wheelbase was most often 48" or 51", on occasion extending to 54" on the original Brill #22 truck. The body was carried by side pads supported by helical springs resting directly on forged side frames, in turn carried by axle boxes via short helical springs. The pads were arcs of a circle around the imaginary pivotal axis as a center, located some 6" to the rear of the leading driving axle.

Brill claimed the 87½% of the weight on the truck was carried on the driving wheels, the load remaining on the pony wheels being "just sufficient to keep them on the track should slight obstructions be encountered."

In subsequent designs the load on drivers was reduced to 75% and even to 60%. Tractive and braking forces were transmitted to the car body through a kingpin secured to the body end sill. The kingpin projected downwards through a block sliding in a radial slot in a casting secured to the head cross-member of the truck frame. There was no bolster and thus, without benefit of swing links, the body was not uncoupled from any action of the truck that was likely to set up unpleasant lateral oscillation.

On straight track the body was carried entirely by the truck side plates. In curves, additional load was placed on the pony wheels by an inverted V-shaped plate attached to the body underframe, the flat extension to each side compressing a helical spring between truck and underframe. As soon as the truck swung into a curve, this shifted load to increase that on the pony wheels to about 30%.

Originally the speed of maximum traction trucks was limited to 30 mph (seldom reached anyway), the laden body weight to 16 tons and the motor power to 50 hp, subsequently raised to 75 hp.

Brill somewhat optimistically claimed that "these Maximum Traction Trucks have superior braking qualities, for the reason that the eight wheels have eight points of friction on the rails and eight brake shoes (while) there was not sufficient friction in the contact of four wheels (of a single-trucker) and track to hold the car." On the other hand, at least one power supply company contended that cars with maximum traction trucks would require more power due to the use of eight wheels. To clear up this point, a commission was set up in 1895, its investigations concluding that "it took no more power to haul a double-truck car than a single-truck car, so we cannot attribute any loss to this feature."

Not satisfied with this, Brill claimed in their 1895 catalog that "Up to 25% is saved in electromotive force over any other truck" and, "This is due to the fact that 87½% of the weight is on the driving wheels, making it practically a four-wheel car, the smaller wheels acting merely as guide wheels; and also for the reason that there is less vibration and oscillation, because of the pivot being outside the center of the truck."

Such claims may have been superfluous, but this was the solution that street railways of 1890-1910 were waiting for and, once available, it was adopted with alacrity by users and makers alike. Early designs varied a great deal in detail, incorporating fabricated, forged or cast frames, helical or laminated springs, or a combination of both, but it was for Brill to come up on top once again, this time with the 39-E truck.

The 39-E used a bolster carried by long, friction-damped hangers and supported by long, laminated springs with helical auxiliaries carried by the spring buckle, while slender forged frame sides were supported by helical axlebox springs. Here was the classic "right" design par excellence! The foot-long hangers, bolster and axlebox springs were in line with the side frames, thus eliminating torsional stresses imposed on the latter.

With this design, the bolster had to be moved nearer to the truck center, reducing the load on the driving wheels but also reducing vertical as well as lateral forces transmitted from the leading wheels to the bolster and thus to the body. Brill also took care to secure the bolster fore and aft to the frame by rubber-bushed links, thus eliminating chatter and rough ride caused by conventional check plates which tended to lock the bolster when starting or stopping. Spring deflection values were not only adequate for the speeds concerned, but also correctly allocated to the bolster and wheelsets; these features took main line railways a long time to understand and still longer to implement!

Dimensions of a typical Brill 39-E truck are shown in the accompanying illustration; less motor, one weighed 4,860 lbs.

Turning the maximum traction truck around so that the pony wheels were outward permitted a floor design gradually dropping towards the end platform. This facilitated passenger circulation, and it also improved riding qualities in and out of curves, since this increased the leverage between the outboard wheels and the truck centers, thus reducing lateral forces transmitted to the car body. In principle then, it would seem better to have both trucks of single-end cars oriented so the pony wheels led, as for example was adopted on quite a few cars of the Cincinnati Street Railway, were it not for the fact that this arrangement was more vulnerable to derailment due to the guided length of the flanges of the small wheels not always being sufficient to bridge the gap at switch or crossing frogs.

A point in favor of the maximum traction truck was made as recently as 1963 by Prof. Dr. Eng H. C. Hermann, the grand old man of rail vehicle running and wheel/rail interaction, who commented that the riding qualities of double-truck cars would be improved if the leading wheels were of smaller diameter than the trailing ones, since this would force a gradual decay of any tendency for a wave-like lateral tracking path.

It has already been noted that during the hey-day of street railways, the maximum traction truck was widely used throughout the world. The Brill 39-E design was adopted with the 1,500 "Nearside" cars of Philadelphia and for hundreds of other U.S. cars. Brill trucks were also chosen for the first 100 London County Council (Municipal) double-deckers, but the remaining 1,600 acquired by this authority used mainly Mountain and Gibson cast steel trucks with LCC-designed bolsters incorporating horizontal coil springs. With London Transport absorbing this, as well as adjoining municipally and privately owned systems, the number of cars with maximum traction trucks in one fleet was well in excess of 2,000!

Berlin introduced maximum traction truck cars in 1896, using GE-800 motors, later changing to GE-67A4 rated 30.4 hp. The trucks were made by Boeker of Remscheid to St. Louis Car Company cast steel frame design. A total of 600 cars were thus equipped by 1912. Many times rebuilt with enclosed platforms, new roofs, magnetic track brakes and 60 hp motors, they lasted until well after World War II. Munich followed suit in 1898, also with St. Louis designed, German-built trucks and 25 hp motors. These continued until 1930 by which time some 500 were in use. Subsequent remotoring made use of 70 hp motors and track brakes were fitted retrospectively in compliance with government requirements.

Birmingham (England) had about 350 cars running on maximum traction trucks with up to 80% of the weight carried on the driving wheels. Glasgow had 150 "standard" cars riding on Kilmarnock-supplied trucks with 54" wheelbase. These were, however, found "not compatible with the local pointwork." Translation: there were embarrassing derailments at the city's busiest junctions, where right angle turns in left-hand traffic had to be negotiated, and "chaos reigned!" Cars had to be reallocated to routes with less demanding track layouts.

Marseille acquired its first car "Americaine a boggie" with Brill #22 truck "avec roues inegales" and GE-1000 motors in 1899, followed in 1905-1908 by another 32, this time with Brill #22 "boggies minimaximum" and GE-57 motors. Brill #22 was also chosen by the Danzig street railway where they ran well into World War II.

From 1900 single-deck and double-deck cars on Brill maximum traction trucks appeared in large numbers in Paris and its suburbs. The Bern (Switzerland) Street Railway in 1901 acquired seven cars on Boeker-supplied St. Louis trucks.

Whatever the numerous variations, the acclaimed original design applied the basic mechanical principle that weight applied to a beam such as the side frame of a truck is transmitted to the axles below in inverse proportion to the displacement of the bolster from those axles. Thus, by offsetting the bolster longitudinally toward the motor wheels and away from the trailer wheels, more weight is put on drive wheels without increasing car weight. Even though not exactly fitting its appellation of Maximum Traction Truck, this insight was due to John A. Brill. It was instrumental in very effectively promoting the rapid acceptance of the double-truck streetcar, in this case powerfully assisted by being able to use just two motors and by avoiding the need of raising car floor levels as required by otherwise available designs.

John A. Brill and his Maximum Traction Truck provided the answer to a pressing need faced by street railways the world over. It would be a wholly fitting recognition of his invention for every transportation museum to preserve a sample of his solution, regardless of its origin, as an example of a simple but effective answer that provided a key step in the evolution of the electric railway industry.

EARLY WORKING CONDITIONS IN RUSSIA AND GERMANY

In the early days of street railways the working conditions of crews were being developed along with the hardware itself. While this volume is illustrative of North American streetcar technology, some reminiscences of operating practices in Russia and in Germany during the 1920s may be of value for comparison.

For example, many Russian undertakings in the south had to run open cars in winter at -20° C (-4° F) with the conductor walking along the car on an outside step to collect fares and the driver standing there swinging both arms against his sides to keep alive. There were not enough closed cars to meet demands and even those had open platforms and little heat in the compartment. Later, a single window pane was mounted in front of the controller as a narrow windshield; the handbrake wheel gearing and linkage would permit no more. So drivers greased their hands and faces, like a channel swimmer!

Handbrakes utilized a screw linkage to develop the leverage needed. A driver had to do up to 15 turns of the wheel to stop the car. This took time, of course, but it did not usually matter as there was no other street traffic to bother about.

The sander was an outside pipe with a funnel at the top and a box full of sand at the dashboard. Sanding was done with the right hand and a scoop.

When the use of trains started after the revolution, about 1923, passengers were allowed to be on the front platform. When they were about to leave some drivers "collected" the fares (no tickets) and split with the conductor. Later, riding on the front platform was reserved for employees and policemen in uniform.

Entrance was strictly at the rear and exit at the front. If one left before the car stopped completely the police fined you on the spot, and they were hot for this as they got 10% of the take!

Russian women were considered then as per the proverb, "Chicken is no bird, woman is not human," but Lenin insisted that women should share in all jobs. Soon they became locomotive enginemen, pilots, sea captains and, of course, streetcar motormen and conductors.

Meal breaks were not provided. Wives met their man's car with a lunch pail of thick soup. This was put on top of the controller and one fed while going along.

Starting signal was two bells (two whistles on open cars), with one bell to stop. Controllers mostly had the OFF position between 10 and 11 o'clock, with full at 6, moving clockwise. Short circuit braking included six or seven notches to the left from OFF down to 6 o'clock; the last used only in emergency for the armature insulation was poor.

Drivers sat on little wooden stools, a la bicycle seats.

In Germany, entrance and exit was at any door. In winter the door between the carbody and the front platform was kept locked, and if someone boarded at the front, the motorman rang the bell to the conductor on the rear platform to indicate that fares were to be collected up front.

Drivers there were issued boots with very thick wooden soles to help resist the cold of winter.

There was dynamic braking for service use, with trailers braked by motor-fed solenoids. At terminals, trailers were shunted into position by hand. (In Russia, one trailer was always left at terminals. An arriving train coupled up to it in front and left behind the one with which it arrived.)

Controllers were similiar to those in Russia, except that Siemens had to be different, starting with OFF at 8 o'clock, series at 11, full ON at 3, and with braking notches from 8 counterclockwise to 3—or even *counterclockwise*, from OFF at 8 to ON at 12, and with braking *clockwise* from 8 to 12! This inversion of normal industry standards for controllers also occured in North American practice, with a property here and there specifying controllers that fed up counterclockwise or brake valves that had inverted quadrants. It persists even today, for example where not all properties agree whether joy-stick type controller handles should be arranged for motoring in forward quadrant and braking in rearward quadrant.

The Germans were conservative in seating the motorman, providing a seat for the first time generally only about 1932, and then so high that the relation of shoulders to controller and brake would be exactly the same whether standing or sitting so that an otherwise different relation might not be used as an excuse in case of an accident.

Until 1933, the London police went one better, with *no* seats and *no* glass at the front of trams (buses as well) to avoid glare in fog and *injury in case of accident!* Some British managers of the day would not have enclosed platforms in any case because "fresh air is good for you!"

On the altruistic side, many German municipal undertakings built large blocks of flats around their carbarns for the accommodation of transit employees. Berlin's Muellerstrasse barn had 300 two or three-room apartments on all three sides and thus made working conditions more acceptable. Today in the States the comparable benefit is a commodious parking lot for employee autos.

J. L. K.

Five-Mile Beach Electric Railway 70

 With its main office at 224 South Michigan Avenue in Chicago, the Five-Mile Beach Electric Railway, operating that much trackage at Wildwood, New Jersey, may have seemed a little elusive. With 17 cars like Jackson & Sharp (AFC)-built #20 ▲ shown here as it appeared in 1943, the little system was a surprise to have existed so recently serving so little permanent population—Wildwood boasted only about 5,300 in 1930!

Photo: O. R. Cummings

Chicago Surface Lines ex-Mail Cars

 At one time carbuilders were willing to tackle orders of only one or two units for special purposes such as for street railway post office service. The two cars shown hauled mail from the middle 1890s until late in 1915 and then went "to pasture" as ► ▲ work cars for another quarter century. Nearest in this 1941 view is #H-202 which had been built for Chicago City Railway, the south side system. Following it is probably #H-1, built for West Chicago Street Railroad and shown here fitted as a platform from which to whitewash carbarn interiors.

Photo: Charles A. Brown

Boston Elevated Railway 20

 Car #995, in center of this 1949 view of Revere barn, had been built by St. Louis Car Company in 1900 for the West End Street Railway, one of 1,202 "25-footers" on that property. When new it had open platforms with just a dasher plate for pro- ► ► tection, but under an order of the legislature, "portable vestibules" were added. The bay window effect permitted full 360° swing of the brake handle. Rebuilt as a service car in 1926.

Photo: Thomas A. Lesh

16

17

D. C Transit System 303

A treasure of early streetcar architecture, Washington's #303 was built in 1898. With an overall length of 25'-6", it has two GE-1000 motors mounted in a Lord Baltimore type truck. Car interiors of the day were finished in handsome contrasting woods; stained glass added a colorful glow to clerestories and wood shutters slid vertically. Shown as it appeared in a 1960 fan trip, #303 is today preserved on public display at the Smithsonian Institution.

Photo: Frank E. Butts

Havana (Camaguey) Electric Railway 9

In 1912, Camaguey (Cuba), then a town of 30,000, received from Brill four arched-roofed single-truck cars. Their wooden underframes were "specially treated with creosote and carbolineum against the inroads of destructive insects." Although their bodies looked like closed cars, they were actually open ones, the side windows being fitted with curtains instead of sash. Heavy tropical rains made ordinary open cars unsatisfactory here. Car #39 shown as it appeared in 1951 was a replacement handed down from the Havana system, where it would have run with double trolleys.

Photo: Francis J. Goldsmith

Tranvias de Matanzas 417

This is how car #417 appeared in 1953 in the north Cuban coastal town of Matanzas, better known to electric railway enthusiasts as the eastern terminal of the Hershey Cuban Railway. There was no track connection between the two companies. Originally built for Havana, #417s 1900 birth date is concealed by subsequent rebuilding.

Photo: J. Wallace Higgins

Ferrocarril Electrico de Torreon 73

Believe it or not, Torreon (Mexico) #73 was built way back in 1906, one of a 20-car lot turned out by American Car Company for Houston, Texas. Four were diverted to El Paso instead. The original monitor-roofed body style was similar to that of San Diego car #1045 shown elsewhere. In the 1940s the El Paso cars were rebuilt to the more modern style seen here and in 1947 they were sold to Torreon. This photo was taken in 1952 during the last few months of their operation.

Photo: J. Wallace Higgins

Chicago Surface Lines 1335

St. Louis Car Company's solution to the "semi-convertible" was its Robertson design, named for its inventor, General Superintendent of Third Avenue Railway, New York City, in the 1890s. Robertson replaced the wooden side truss framing previously concealed in each car side with a steel channel sill running the length of the body and a simple framing of bars. This opened up space for sash to drop between window posts.

▲ Upper photo shows version supplied in quantity to Chicago City Railway in 1901-1902, as it looked operating on 111th Street in May 1941.

▼ Lower view, taken on the Cermak-Lawndale shuttle line in 1942, shows smaller type (not Robertson) built for Chicago Union Traction in 1903 and 1906.

Photos: Charles A. Brown

Louisville Railway 805

Contemporary production of 1902 included 75 cars (800-874) built for Louisville by the St. Louis Car Company. They had a 28' long compartment and rode on DuPont #24 trucks. Seen here at Western Parkway on the Market Street line in 1946.

Photo: George G. McKinley

The City Railway Company 72

E. J. Barney was a vice-president of The City Railway of Dayton, Ohio, when another contemporary streetcar (and railroad coach) builder was the local plant of The Barney & Smith Car Co. In 1903 they produced car #72, shown in lower photo taken in 1939. Notice the concave-convex side panels, a styling idea that weaves in and out of streetcar design repeatedly from horsecar days to the present.

Photo: by Frank M. Brown from C.A. Smallwood collection

21

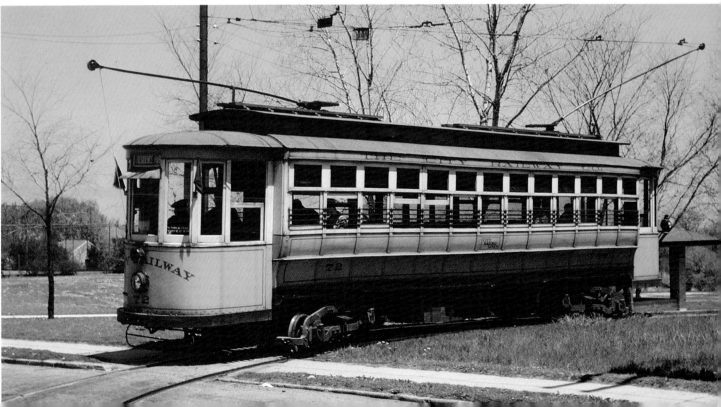

Market Street Railway 1572

▲ In this photo, taken at 12th and Mission Streets in July 1946, is recorded one of San Francisco's distinctive and heavy old-timers. When delivered in 1906 they had an unusual air brake system, with duplicate brake valves and rigging to operate wood track brake shoes. They were rebuilt in 1911 for pay-as-you-enter fare collection. A few survived until 1949.

Photo: by A. R. Alter, from Bill Billings collection

Mexico City Tramways, Ltd. 880

◄ An example of a high-capacity wood-bodied street car built in the first decade of the twentieth century. Not so typical for urban service was the train operation with multiple-unit control as seen in this view, taken in 1953 at the end of the line in Xochimilco. These cars were retired in 1956, after a half-century of service.

Photo: J. Wallace Higgins

Chicago Transit Authority 133

◄◄ One of an order of 600 "Big Pullmans" built in 1908-1909 for Chicago Railways Company. They introduced the Pay-As-You-Enter (PAYE) concept to the north side system. The heaviest streetcars in Chicago, they weighed 54,000 lbs. and were 40 ft. long. In the background of this 1950s photo is Montgomery Ward's building, Larrabee at Chicago Avenues.

Photo: Glenn M. Andersen

San Diego Electric Railway 1045
The J. G. Brill Company of Philadelphia offered a "semi-convertible" car design in the early 1900s, when the seasonal allure of separate open and closed cars was at its peak. Brill's patent covered its "grooveless post" system in which *both* the upper and lower sash could be raised into a pocket formed between the roof and a curved interior ceiling liner. A competing approach was to drop the lower sash into a side pocket, but this resulted in narrowing the useful floor space if a truss frame was built into the side between the sills and the belt rail as was normal construction of the time.

This photo, dating to 1946, recorded #1045, one of 26 cars acquired in 1942 by San Diego from the Third Avenue Railway of New York City. It helped meet burgeoning wartime traffic in the home base city of the U.S. Pacific fleet.

Photo: by A. R. Alter, from Bill Billings collection

Los Angeles Transit Lines 611

The "California" car plan combined open and closed sections into one carbody. The first cars of this plan seem to have been built for the California Street Cable Railroad of San Francisco. Los Angeles adopted a similar arrangement for what turned out to be 747 "Type B Standards" acquired over the next ten years. One of them, #611, is shown in 1946 in the livery of the Los Angeles Transit Lines, a color scheme shared with other systems coast to coast that were then managed by the National City Lines Organization.

Photo: by A. R. Alter, from Bill Billings collection

25

Sioux City Service Company 16

From the early 1900s until after World War II, streetcar technology was such that building car bodies and equipping them was within the capability of enterprising master mechanics such as Charles M. Feist of Sioux City, Iowa. Here is one of his products standing in front of its birthplace in June 1948.

Photo: Lawson K. Hill

THE "PAY-AS-YOU-ENTER" CAR
A revolutionary solution to the problem of passenger handling

The rapid growth of cities fostered by the introduction of electric railways with their relatively high speed compared to then-existing horse or mule-drawn vehicles resulted in a sharp increase of traffic density and a need for more efficient utilization of cars and crews. Larger cars made it urgently necessary to improve the prevailing fare collection system, wherein the conductor had to wait for the passengers to find their seats or standing spaces before paying each a personal visit to settle the fare. Not just tiring, this slowed the service and was vulnerable to cheating. During rush hours, conscientious conductors had to push their way through the standees to the rear platform before giving the starting bell, only to have to shove back again to get more fares.

This method of operation dated from more leisurely horsecar days but productivity experts, impressed by the "American system of manufacture" sought a system resembling the conveyor belt assembly line, with passengers moving past a conductor working in a fixed location where fares would be collected and tickets issued. That much was obvious but the challenge was how to achieve it.

The first fundamentally correct solution was demonstrated on May 4, 1905 by the Montreal Street Railway when it introduced car number 890 (later renumbered #900), the original prepayment or pay inside car, identified by its designers as "Pay-As-You-Enter" (PAYE) car.

For almost ten years the PAYE plan became the standard accepted by most North American street railway operators. Actually, the basic PAYE method of fare collection was fundamentally not new, having been tried by one or two companies but found wanting since then-prevailing car designs were not suitable for it. Montreal made the idea practical by lengthening the rear platform and rearranging the doors connecting it to the main car body.

The ideas incorporated in the Montreal car were credited by some as being triggered by the large rear platform Detroit had adopted for its cars. Others ascribe the Montreal concept to a local conductor or to a student at McGill University, but whatever its origin, implementation was due to two leading officials of the Montreal Street Railway.

The adopted solution is best described by Blake and Jackson in their textbook, "Electric Railway Transportation," published by McGraw-Hill in 1917. Henry W. Blake, once engineer with Frank J. Sprague (the "father" of electric traction) was the distinguished editor of the influential "Electric Railway Journal" from 1891 to 1925. Walter Jackson was a prominent electric railway consultant of the time. In a chapter entitled "Car Types in Relation to Traffic," they come straight to the point. Quoting:

"Up to 1905, the doors and steps of city electric cars showed no radical advance over those of horse-car days. A few cars for rapid transit service had been built entirely of steel, but the art of city car design seemed to have gone the way of Tyrian purple and tempered bronze. But in that year a pair of courageous Canadians, W. G. Ross and Duncan McDonald, then respectively managing director and superintendent of the Montreal Street Railway Company, showed a skeptical street railway world that pay-as-you-enter (prepayment) fare collection really was practicable. All they did to revolutionize fare collection was to lengthen the conductor's platform, installing dividing rails, provide two doors instead of one in the rear bulkhead, one an inwardly opening door for entrance, and the other an outwardly opening door for exit, and, finally, supply also a front exit door under the control of the motorman. Chicago, New York and other cities followed Montreal in rapid order. With each installation came many new conveniences quite foreign to the question of prepayment itself. The electric railways were now eager to adopt a system of collection which would intercept fares previously missed and which, by keeping the conductor on the platform, would also avoid many boarding and alighting accidents. They feared, however, that the public would refuse to accept the new or rebuilt prepayment cars unless they showed manifest superiority in convenience and safety. Thus began an era of improvement which even after a decade is still in full vigor. Prepayment, therefore, is directly responsible for the use of larger platforms, wider aisles, inter-operating doors and steps and many safety devices. . . ."

The conductor stood or sat mostly with his back to the partition separating the platform from the interior. Entrance was on the right side at the very rear of the car, past the fare-taking conductor and through a swinging door to the inside. Exit was optionally from the rear or front platform, using sliding doors with short access aisles along the right hand side of the interior, not affecting the conductor at the rear or the passengers at the front. Typically, when boarding a group of passengers the conductor would immediately begin collecting fares from the queue forming and continue doing so until some passenger offered silver or currency exceeding the fare. Then the conductor would grab the bell cord and divert his attention to observing the rear step, relying on the rider waiting for change to hold the queue. As soon as the conductor saw that boarding and alighting at the rear was complete, he would sound the two-bells "go ahead" for the motorman and resume fare collection.

The first Montreal PAYE cars were 42'-3" long with 7'-6" platform. On later cars the overall length was increased to 44'-4" and even 46'-4", both with 7'-6" platform, while one car, 940, was 51'-10" long and had 9'-6" platform! In this car, the body was offset 2¾" to the right relative to the trucks to provide curve clearance, but even so, it was the rule that certain cars not pass one another on sharp curves. The cars were generally a generous 8'-9¾" wide. Most seated 44 and accommodated another 60 standees. Typical European operation of that time would have required one four-wheel motor car with two trailers and a crew of four to provide equivalent capacity, a practice adhered to right up until the end of World War II.

In September 1906 Montreal 940 was shown at the convention of the American Street Railway Association in Columbus, Ohio, where it attracted much favorable attention. As compared to existing fare collection practices of the day, it was conceded that PAYE might cost a little time at a few very heavy boarding points but it was expected that these losses would be recouped at the more typical stops.

Some passengers were at first offended at being expected to pay before being allowed to enter the car, impugning, they felt, their ability or intention to pay. Some local papers used this to make fun of the PAYE system, but this didn't last.

It became obvious that Ross and McDonald were on to a good thing. Shortly the patent-holding Pay-As-You-Enter Car Corporation was established on Church Street, New York, seat of many leading consultants and street railway holding companies. McDonald was President. Car builders and transit operators were queueing up for licenses to build or rebuild in accordance with the highly successful PAYE arrangement. Improvements that made it even more attractive included power-operated platform doors and folding steps. These permitted elimination of the bulkhead and introduced the "sun-parlor" concept. The sliding front exit door was located well forward to the front right corner post so that the motorman had scarcely to turn his head when observing alighting passengers.

In the United States it was Thomas E. Mitten, then President of the Chicago City Railways, who first introduced PAYE cars by a 1907 order of three hundred 45'-9" long by 9'-0" wide cars, seating 44, with the conductors instructed not to carry more than a total of 80. These cars were hailed as a "remarkable success, probably the most important achievement in the history of electric railways for the year 1907!" As claimed at the time by the City Railway, "The Pay-As-You-Enter system which is on trial here for the first time in the U.S., thus places men in command of platforms. The plan is not a mere nickel-grabbing, turnstile device—it is primarily and essentially a life and limb saver."

This somewhat sweepingly altruistic claim was once more stressed by Mitten in his report to the Mayor of Chicago of September 1908, in which he stated: "The fatal accidents were one to every 4,172,727 passengers carried, as against one to every 2,596,919 during the same period last year. Accidents (other than fatal) show a decrease of 16.2%, with almost entire elimination of that class of accidents sustained in boarding or leaving the front platform."

27

The Chicago Railways Company (serving the other half of Chicago then) followed a year later, acquiring 600 similar cars, which by 1911 increased to 1,328. New York Railways purchased 155. Altogether some 4,000 were built or rebuilt from existing stock by 1909 and in Chicago alone over 2,000 were acquired up to 1915.

PAYE car length ranged between 41' in Washington to 50' in Cleveland and in Milwaukee. Width varied 8'-0" to 9'-0". Number of seats ranged from 40 in Chicago to 56 in Pittsburgh, car weight between 32,250 lb. in Washington to 53,000 lb. in Boston.

Installed motor power ranged between 100 and 200 hp respectively, or 6 to 7½ hp per ton. The important platform length could be as little as 6' with the Third Avenue cars up to 7'-8" in Cleveland, where smokers were confined to the rear platform or to the left of the front one.

The smooth conquest of obsolete operating methods by the "conveyor belt" concept of the Pay-As-You-Enter Car Corporation was temporarily interrupted by Mitten's sponsorship of the "Nearside" car in Buffalo, Philadelphia and Chicago. However, until the advent of Peter Witt's all-conquering Cleveland solution, the PAYE car remained the undisputed leader in a field which it made predominantly its own for almost ten lucrative years.

J. L. K.

THREE STREET RAILWAY PIONEERS
Originally prepared for *Strassenbahn Magazin*
Edited by CERA for presentation in English

Thomas E. Mitten

In the early days of horsecars, it was common for passengers to enter those small vehicles at the rear and pass their fares up to the driver, sometimes via a metal chute along the window posts. As traffic increased cars got bigger. Doors were provided at *both* ends for street access for boarding and alighting. A conductor was employed on each car with the principal task of searching out each boarding rider and collecting the fare. When still larger double-truck cars came into use the problems of chasing down each additional passenger became unacceptable. On trips where the cars were tightly packed with standees, the weakness of the pay-anywhere plan of fare collection was painfully evident, causing intolerable delay and fare abuse. Inventive minds in the street railway industry began looking for better ideas.

In 1905 the Montreal Tramways developed the first successful "Pay-as-you-enter" (PAYE) car, proving that it was practical for a crew of two to handle a hundred or more passengers, including collecting their fares systematically. In the PAYE design all passengers entered at the rear where the conductor was stationed, paying their fares to pass him. Alighting was permitted at either end of the car. The Pay-As-You-Enter Car Corporation held patents on the design, but did not build cars. Instead it licensed its design to carbuilders or street railway companies who built (or in some cases, rebuilt) the cars.

Some users were still not quite satisfied with the PAYE solution, since, while the conductor was busy with boarding passengers, the motorman often had nothing to do but wait for the starting bell, and while the car was running between stops the conductor had little to do. Also, many car stops had been located near side (i.e., *before* the street crossing), which presumably made access more convenient considering the many unpaved streets of the day, especially if one could board either end of the car. Unfortunately, under the new PAYE plan a passenger might be forced to walk through mud and dirt to board at the rear. A better arrangement might speed up service and it was to meet this challenge that the "Nearside" car was developed by Thomas E. Mitten in 1910.

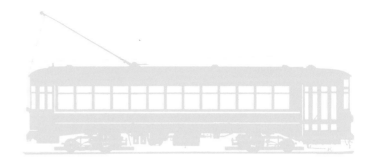

At this period of American history, the industry formed by the suppliers and operators of street, interurban, subway and elevated railways was a very important part of the nation's economy. The number of vehicles acquired by just the street and interurban railways during the 1907-1910 period, shown in the following table, illustrates this point:

	1907	1908	1909	1910
Street railway cars	3483	2208	2537	3571
Interurban railway cars	1327	727	1245	990
Freight and work cars	1406	176	1175	820
Totals	6216	3111	4957	5381

Of the cars built in 1909, no less than 1096 were of the PAYE type, while in 1910 this increased to 1878! In addition, some 1200 miles of new track had been built in 1908, 837 in 1909 and 1271 in 1910. It surely was a rapidly growing industry and if, as did Whitney in Boston, Huntington in Los Angeles or Spreckels in San Diego, one combined the building of street and interurban railways with purchase (and later on, selling) of land, then it was possible to get quite wealthy in a very short time indeed!

In 1910 there were 1279 companies in the USA, with 40,300 miles of track and 89,601 cars; by 1912 their number was down to 1209 but the mileage was up slightly to 40,610 using 91,457 vehicles. By 1923, further consolidation had brought the number of undertakings down to 823, but there were 46,810 miles of track and 105,046 cars. It was the country's fifth largest business.

Now the story returns to Mitten. Coming with his parents from his birthplace in Brighton, Sussex, in England, Thomas E. Mitten (1865-1929) at the age of eight settled on a farm in Newton County, Indiana, where in his free time he was allowed to operate the telegraph at the Chicago & Eastern Illinois Railroad station at Goodland. In 1885 he was entrusted with running a whole station, albeit one consisting of an old freight car. From 1887 to 1890 he was running a slightly larger station, but health considerations now forced him to move westward.

From 1893 to 1896 he managed the newly electrified interurban from Denver to Golden in Colorado and then moved to Milwaukee to become assistant superintendent and later general superintendent of The Milwaukee Electric Railway & Light Company. In 1901 he moved to Buffalo to take up duties of the general superintendent of International Railways' street railway system on the eve of the great Pan-American Exposition. His superb handling of the heavy traffic generated by that exposition earned him a promotion to the post of General Manager.

In 1905 he became president of Chicago City Railway, operator of a large network of street railways serving the south side of Chicago, but retaining his connection with Buffalo by becoming vice-president and a director. In 1911 he became a director and chairman of the executive committee of the Philadelphia Rapid Transit Company, formed of ten then-existing street railways and the Market Street Elevated. Giving as his reason the press of these new duties, he resigned his Chicago post (but not his Buffalo connections) effective December 30, 1911. The new PRT organization embraced some 620 miles of track, 2746 motor cars and 91 trailers.

About this time, he also founded Mitten Management to provide services for both Philadelphia and Buffalo, the latter then including some 418 miles of track, 827 motor and 23 trail cars.

Since the PAYE cars of Buffalo were not entirely satisfactory, Mitten, with Ralph T. Senter (International's master mechanic and future PRT general manager), evolved the "Nearside" car solution, in which the entrance and exit as well as *both* the motorman and conductor were placed at the front end. There were adjoining folding doors here, the forward being used for entrance with exit through the rearmost. Fare was paid when passing the conductor, who was a little behind the motorman along the left side of the car. The front platform could hold 10-15 passengers, so the car could resume movement before the conductor had collected all the fares.

Although the cars had air brakes, the doors were manually operated by the motorman as Mitten was concerned that air door operating mechanisms might freeze up in Buffalo's severe winters. Mitten also insisted on the entrance doors folding inward and the exit doors folding outward. Incidentally, an important advantage expected of the design was that the conductor's working environment would be improved by being in the heated car body rather than on an open platform and the motorman, too, would have a better heated area than in the PAYE car.

To facilitate passenger circulation, longitudinal seats were provided through the forward part of the car while cross seats were used in the rear. A single folding door was provided at the extreme rear of the right side, manually operated from the conductor's stand, to be used with "crush" loads and to speed up passenger exit at terminals.

Mitten was very conscious of the need to keep the cars clean and insisted on the use of wood slat seats as well as rounded inside corners. Straps for standees were covered with washable celluloid and since tobacco chewing was a contemporary problem, interiors were painted a deep brown to match! Air circulation was supplemented by intake openings at floor level and exhaust ventilators on the roof. Dr. W. A. Evans, health commissioner of Chicago was an advisor in that area.

In operation, motormen stopped their cars abreast of intersecting crosswalks, operated the front doors for passenger boarding and alighting, then closed them and proceeded without waiting for a signal from the conductor, who in the meantime carried on with fare collection as needed. The company's statements stressed that it was a special advantage of the new layout that it avoided the need for passengers to alight and then cross the road at the rear in the face of oncoming traffic.

Buffalo was the first town to receive "Nearside" cars and got 364 of them. It was followed by Chicago with 125. The topper was Philadelphia, which obtained no less than 1500 between 1911 and 1913, probably the largest single procurement of any one type car in all transit history! An order of 26 was supplied to the Atlantic City & Shore Railway, one to Lincoln (Nebraska) and a left-hand sample to Vancouver (British Columbia). All were built by J. G. Brill Company at its home plant in Philadelphia or subsidiary G. C. Kuhlman plant in Collingwood (Cleveland).

The "Nearside" cars were 45'-2" long, 8'-6" wide and 12' high. They weighed only 39,000 lb. (736 lb. per passenger for 53 seats). They rested on Brill 39-E maximum traction trucks and were powered with 2 - 45 kw motors (Wh 306) using single end K-36 control. The low entrance design was ensured by arranging the trucks to operate with pony (trailer) wheels outward, permitting the floor level to drop by nearly 3½" from the kingpin towards the front platform. This had one 11" followed by two 13¼" steps leading down to pavement.

The entrance door was 28¾" wide, the exit door 24¾", and the emergency rear door, 26⅝". With 35" wide cross seats, the center aisle was 27" wide, increasing to 55½" between the forward longitudinal seats. While the front platform had an interior length of about six feet, with the space taken up by the crew, their controls and separating railings, there remained effectively space inside the car for only a few persons waiting to pay fare.

It soon became apparent that the new cars did not meet all expectations. Uneven distribution of riders through the car was a constant problem. During rush hours conductors were known to climb on their seat to plead with passengers to move to the rear. Once a "Nearside" was loaded (up to 150 people could jam into one!) it became time consuming and irritating to get off. The rear emergency exit door had to be operated more frequently than anticipated, since people couldn't be expected to fight their way some 45 ft. to the rear and then all the way forward to alight at the front. The rear door, which was fitted with a horizontally pivoted rollover step (like Buffalo's new LRV's but without any of today's safety devices), had no handrails and it was nearly impossible to observe from the front end to know when to close and start the car.

The floor-level air intakes caused complaints of drafts and unpleasant odors, the latter arising from horse-drawn traffic of the day. New air intakes were placed on the roof near each end of the car.

The close proximity of the conductor and motorman encouraged distracting conversation between them and this, with the shortage of buffer space for riders waiting to pay fare led to consideration of moving the conductor a little toward the rear. Apparently Philadelphia made this change in 1913 at a cost of three seats. Chicago considered the idea but didn't make the change.

In the period 1919-1921, 1160 of Philadelphia's "Nearsides" were rebuilt to include a centrally located double-stream exit door with the conductor adjacent. The management at the time stated that door control technology had advanced to make the change safe. Subsequent experience showed that the improvement to passenger flow reduced stopping times by some 10%.

Philadelphia called its design the "Public Service Car" although it was conceptually equivalent to the Peter Witt design developed in Cleveland. Eventually Philadelphia's cars were further changed to permit one-person operation and remained in service until the mid-1950s. Buffalo did not modify its "Nearsides", except for one-manning. Neither did Chicago, but follow-on orders there used much of the basic design modified with a rear vertibule and double end layout.

A single-truck version of the "Nearside" design was also built in 1912 for use on International Railway's Lockport local lines. Similar single-truckers went to Manistee (Michigan) and Sorocaba (Brazil) among other places.

Although the "Nearside" car was not repeated, the one-man solution influenced the evolution of the Birney Safety Car, of which some 6,000 were acquired by street railways. Thomas Mitten's interest in PAYE and "Nearside" cars have made a permanent imprint on public transit technology. His inventiveness and willingness to try new ideas truly qualify him as a street railway pioneer.

Frank Hedley

Frank Hedley was born in 1864 in England. He trained as a machinist before emigrating to the USA in 1882, where for two years he was employed in the shops of the Erie and New York Central Railroads. Next he became a machinist with the Manhattan Elevated Railway and in 1885 he became assistant general foreman of the locomotive department. In 1889 he was appointed master mechanic of the Kings County Elevated Railroad of Brooklyn, but in 1893 he left to accept the post of superintendent of motive power for the Lake Street Elevated Railroad at Chicago. Within a few months he was made general superintendent.

This newly-built line was controlled by traction tycoon Charles T. Yerkes. Between 1893 and 1896 it was operated with 35 Forney 0-4-4 type two-cylinder compound steam locomotives built by the Rhode Island Locomotive Works and 125 light wooden coaches built by Gilbert and Pullman plants. During 1895-1896, 38 of the trail coaches were fitted with two 92 kw motors each, arranged to work as locomotive cars pulling trailers and the road changed over to electric operation. Multiple unit control, invented by Frank J. Sprague, did not appear before 1897.

Less than two years after going to Chicago, Hedley was appointed consulting engineer by Yerkes, so that in addition to his existing duties he could devote himself to problems associated with the construction of the Northwestern Elevated and the Chicago Union Loop, the former being provided with sixty 2 x 120 kw motor cars and 160 trailers. He also advised Yerkes in connection with the design of cars for another Yerkes project, the London Underground.

In January 1903 Hedley was made general superintendent of Manhattan's Interborough Rapid Transit Company and the following year became general manager of that organization, which by that time employed a staff of 18,500. In 1908 he was elected vice president and general manager, responsible for operation of all elevated and subway lines in Manhattan, the Bronx and part of Brooklyn. These lines embraced 360 miles of track with 2858 motor and 1382 trail cars.

Hedley's responsibilities rose and with them came top salary of the day for the industry, $75,000! Yet, he was of the opinion that "any fool could be president of a railroad company, but the general manager has to know something!" He was aiming at high corporate earnings and low expenditure. When his attention was drawn to the poor condition of the rolling stock, he stated that it could not be otherwise as long as the city insisted on the 5-cent fare. "I saw a car with clean windows today and when I got back to the office, I raised hell to find out who spent all the money!" was his response. He was rather contemptuous of conferences and commissions: his method followed the simpler procedure of "I will study the situation and then do as I please."

While still in Chicago he developed a truck design which, even by today's standards, can be considered modern. It has been used in New York, London, and Los Angeles as well as Chicago. He was the inventor of the widely-used anti-climber, a three-lipped channel attached to car end sills to constrain overriding of one car over the next in event of collision. In New York, he introduced the first air-operated side doors. Another Hedley gadget was a "Free-wheeling Indicator" he developed to encourage motormen to reduce current consumption.

When the Metropolitan Street Railway, operating over 300 track miles in Manhattan, was dissolved, the Interborough took over about 70 miles of it with 1700 cars. Under the name New York Railways, Hedley was appointed vice president and general manager, with a staff of about 8,500.

Because of bad experience with ruthless and dangerous installations of overhead electric wires, Manhattan forbad any such further use and the street railways had to resort to underground current collection. As usual, Hedley got "a better idea" from this.

The problem presented Hedley with a chance to evolve, with New York Railway's rolling stock engineer, J. S. Doyle, a street car which would meet all of the then prevailing requirements. Hedley interpreted this to demand a low floor car with a through-running stepless floor. The result was, according to the Electric Railway Journal, " . . . a car which is unquestionably the most radical departure from accepted tradition of street railway practice which has ever been attempted," without, however, mentioning that somewhat similar cars were supplied by Siemens in 1896 for the Budapest subway.

The reasons leading to the new stepless design included rapid passenger interchange, reduced stopping times and consequently higher schedule speeds as well as increased line capacity. Styles for ladies' dresses in 1910 demanded long, close-fitting skirts which only permitted short steps. High steps could be negotiated, but it meant lifting the skirt to what was then considered an indiscreet height! The new car, with a step height of only 10", avoided the difficulties. Further advantages claimed at the time included comfortable seats, a fixed conductor position with improved working conditions, enameled tubular grabrails and stanchions, conductor-operated air doors,

separated motorman's compartment, eight natural draft ventilators, warm air heating, rounded car ends able to push aside road vehicles, smooth outside body surface (discouraging hangers-on) and short distance from door to seats assured by the center entrance. Of course, some of these advantages have been cited over the years by proponents of center entrance cars.

It is interesting to note that the general plans for the first "stepless" car were received at the J. G. Brill Car works on Thursday evening, February 29, 1912 and on the following Friday, the car and trucks were photographed and shipped. They were described by the local press on March 16 and put into operation on March 21 . . . was it really a better world in those days?

The new 16 ton car provided space for 51 seated and 38 standing passengers. The maximum traction trucks carried one 37.5 kw motor each, mounted toward the outside. Having the driving wheels leading could not have been conducive to smooth entry and exit from the transition-less street railway curves. The side doors were interlocked with the control, and the driver could put the controller on the first point and let the conductor start the car by closing the doors, a timesaving arrangement that is commonly used on light and heavy rail transit today. The driver's cab was a little cramped and its sole entrance from the outside of the car was inconvenient and drafty.

The maximum traction truck as evolved by John Albert Brill (1852-1908) and similar designs were noteworthy for their masterly, practical, robust and undemanding construction. The slim forged steel longitudinal members permitted the placement of axleboxes and bolster springs directly below them so that they were not subject to torsional stresses. The 69" lateral spacing of bolster leaf springs ensured effective resistance against body swaying. As compared for example to the standard of 1.2 meters for 1941 German cars, this means that, with identical spring stiffness, the Brill truck of 1911 offered more than twice greater resistance to swaying.

The car body was carried on foot-long swing links which effectively decoupled the car body from the sinusoidal truck oscillations which develop as a car moves down the track. The total springing corresponded to the simple rule (based on extensive investigations) calling for about 1/10" deflection per mph of free speed, or approximately 3" total spring deflection at 30 mph. Of this deflection, about a quarter should be allocated to the axlebox springs. A higher value can cause undue truck frame pitching and longitudinal jerking of the car body. With the Brill trucks, the laminated bolster springs provided about 1¼"; the bolster beam coil spring another 7/8" and the axlebox springs about 5/8".

Since truck pitching oscillations could cause body fore-and-aft jerking due to the action of check plates which also restrain free bolster up-and-down motion when accelerating or braking, Brill replaced these by securing the bolster longitudinally with the aid of rubber bushed links. Truck nosing could be reduced by restraining forces emanating from the car body. However, certain limits must be observed here to prevent undue wear of railheads and wheel flanges, even the risk of derailment. The problem must be solved by having "not too little nor too much."

Investigations carried out by the writer some thirty years ago showed that these requirements will be met if X (the restraining torque in ton-meters) = 0.03 to 0.05, with wheelbase measured in meters and axle load in metric tons. This requirement was met by the Brill trucks supplied for the Mitten "Nearside" cars and those for the Hedley-Doyle cars.

The New York management considered the new low-floor cars successful enough so that, still within 1912, another 175 were acquired, however, this time the motorman's cab was extended. The cars soon became known as the "Broadway Battleships."

Before the end of 1912, one sample "Stepless" was delivered to Vancouver (British Columbia) which at the same time began testing a Mitten "Nearside." In the following year 35 similar cars were bought by the Southern Pacific for use on its Pacific Electric lines in Pasadena, and for its other subsidiaries in Fresno, San Jose and Stockton. The twenty assigned to PE received multiple unit control, while the remainder got 4 S + 4 P (= 4 steps in series + 4 in parallel) K-type platform controllers.

The cars found little favor in California, where they were known as the "dragons," partly because of the weak front end which came off badly even in collision with older wooden cars. Since they couldn't practically be converted for one-man operation, all were withdrawn by 1934. For similar reasons, the New York cars had already been replaced by much older cars that could be and were changed for one-man operation.

Encouraged by the local success of their "Stepless" car, a somewhat similar double-deck version was evolved by Hedley and Doyle, with an order for one being placed with Brill. It had to be rather low to clear numerous elevated viaducts. First runs were made on Broadway on August 14, 1912. The 23-ton car was powered by 2x41 kw motors and provided 44 seats on each deck for a total, with standees, of 171! However, because of slow loading/unloading this car remained a one-of-a-kind venture.

On the other hand, a somewhat similar car, 13'-1" high, was obtained by the Columbus (Ohio) Railway, Power & Light Company in 1914 in an effort to reduce traffic congestion on the main thoroughfare, traversed by ten street car lines. This acquisition was justified by the following data:

Type of car:	Double-deck	Single car	Two cars M+M	Two cars M+T
No. of seats	83	40	80	100
Tare wt., lb.	46,000	35,773	71,546	61,773
Costs: ¢/mile	11.121	9.526	16.483	15.232

The Hedley-Doyle double-deck car was chosen because of greater safety, low entrance, reduced street occupancy and low operating costs per mile. Nevertheless, no repeat orders followed.

A year later the Vienna street railway tried their luck with two somewhat similar cars having an unusual seating arrangement. Known as type F, they weighed about 24 tons. They had space for 56 seated and 30 standing passengers. A special bow current collector permitted passage under low viaducts. However, experience with these cars was not deemed satisfactory and so it was left to England (and countries under its influence) to remain favoring the use of double-deckers. Perhaps this was in part because the British were used to climbing stairs in their two-story one-family houses. Also, passenger standing in street cars and buses was hampered by trade unions and the police.

Since the traffic density of the short transverse lines on Manhattan Island did not justify the cost of underground conduit power distribution, when it came time to replace horse cars, storage battery vehicles were introduced. These were small four-wheelers, some 116 of which were operated by New York Railways, while another 340 were used by the neighboring Third Avenue Railway and its subsidiaries. Here too Hedley made use of the "Stepless" idea as incorporated in a new four-wheeler built by Brill towards the end of 1912. This vehicle weighed less than five tons without its electrical equipment. It seated 34 and had standing space for 28 more. It was powered by 44 battery cells placed under the longitudinal seats. Two motors, placed under the transverse seats, drove the nearest axle through chains. The cars, which remained in service until 1933, were somewhat similar to Berlin trailers that were originally fitted with individually rotating wheels to give low floor. These had been replaced with conventional wheel sets in 1933.

Peter Witt

As far as street railways were concerned, the career of Peter Witt (born 1869) was essentially of the consulting type, but its results have been retained far better than those of many leading personalities in this field. Witt came from Cleveland, which at the time had about 650,000 inhabitants. He became city clerk during the administration of Mayor Tom L. Johnson from 1903 to 1910. The city clerk at that time was the top administrator for the city while the mayor dealt with the politics, representations and civic functions. Johnson, who controlled a number of street railways, devoted himself to business policies and won election in part by campaigning for reduction of the local fare from 5¢ to 3¢ (an unusual cause for an owner of street railways).

Witt's knowledge of taxation and kindred subjects led Johnson to appoint him head of a tax investigation. In 1912 he was made street railway commissioner by Mayor Baker. His duties included planning and supervision of extensions, routing, schedules, fares, ordinances controlling street trackage and car operation in general. The local system at the time included 1034 motor and 444 trail cars operating over some 372 miles of track.

After 1916 Witt acted as consultant to the Van Sweringen brothers, prominent real estate developers, who had in the meantime acquired control of the Cleveland street railways and a number of main line railroad undertakings only to enter receivership soon afterwards.

Witt originated the alternate-stop plan. It increased schedule speed by about two mph and encouraged the use of center door trailers. In 1914-1915 the company acquired another 199 center entrance motor cars. These were 51' long and had 59 seats. They were very popular with the crews due to the significant reduction in drafts.

Originally the cars had a flat, low-level vestibule floor with steps fore and aft leading to the main car floor. This gave problems, particularly in rush periods, as all too often riders were thrown against the steps during acceleration and braking. To avoid this, the area was modified by running the car floor at a common level throughout with steps leading to the doors only. Having made this change, the area at the conductor's position proved inadequate to buffer boarding passengers waiting to pay fares in rush hours at heavy interchange stops.

The need to obtain new rolling stock led Witt to find a combined solution for the two interrelated problems. In the car design which has come to bear his name he sought to provide low-friction passenger interchange and a large "catchment area." He found a way to provide both by superimposing a center exit door on a "Nearside" floor plan and relocating the conductor position from the front vestibule (as in Mitten's plan) to a location adjacent to that center door. With this layout, a motorman could stop the car exactly next to boarding passengers where he could monitor the boarding. Passengers would have substantial buffer space between the longitudinal seats extending from the front to the center doors. Exit was permitted only at the center door, where riders paid fares and then had the choice of alighting or continuing into the rear half of the car, which was fitted with transverse seats, to ride on to their destination.

The first "pay-as-you-pass" car (referred to in Cleveland as "Pete's Pet") appeared on December 1, 1914 on the Harvard-Denison line which connected southern suburbs in an eight-mile semi-circle.

Usually the line was served by 19 cars and it required 42-47 minutes for the trip. A number of radial lines presenting heavy transfer traffic were crossed within a distance of about three miles. Witt saw that full separation of boarding from alighting would substantially speed up service.

The new cars, in which Witt was assisted in engineering of detail by Terence Scullin, Cleveland Railway master mechanic, were 51' long, 8'-2" wide and weighed about 23 tons. They provide 55 seats and standing room for another 77. They were powered with 4x36 kw motors. The entrance door at front was 44" wide, while the center exit had two streams, each 33⅜" wide.

The new design was an immediate and resounding success. Fifty cars were ordered in 1915 followed by another 80 in 1916. The design superseded PAYE plan in most orders. It could be modified for use in southern states, where at that time passengers were segregated by race. Birmingham, Alabama, under two-man crew operation required blacks to board and alight at the center and to ride in the rear, where longitudinal seating was provided. Whites boarded at the center and alighted in the front. The forward part of the car had cross seats. Segregated seating has, of course, been outlawed for a full generation now.

Experience and measurement confirmed that cars built in accordance with Peter Witt's principles ensured higher schedule speeds and improved working conditions. His solution became an industry standard and was carried over into later President's Conference Committee (PCC) street cars, buses and trolley buses, without, however, giving Witt's name the general credit due it. With the advent of one-man operation, the Peter Witt design was quite adaptable to elimination of the conductor and relocation of fare collection to the front platform where the motorman of earlier times became the "operator" of the new day.

And so the three pioneers, Mitten, Hedley and Witt, each in his own way, contributed substantially to the development of city transportation, a fact we are pleased to commemorate here.

J. L. K.

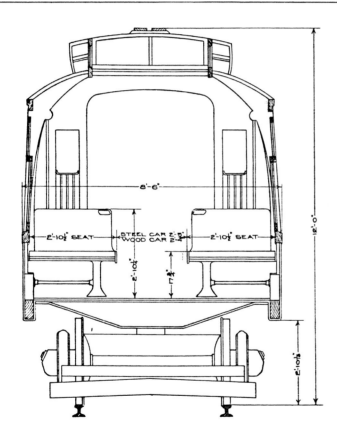

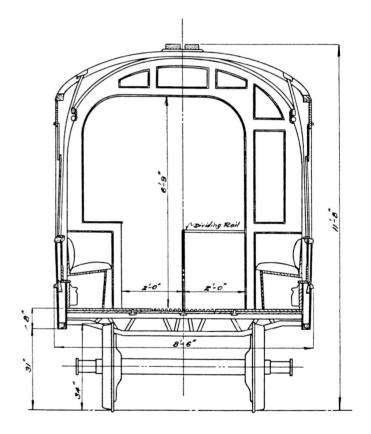

Comparative Cross-Sections of Alternative Designs
▲ Brill's Patented "Semi-Convertible" car for the Boston Elevated Railway, 1908

Mitten's "Nearside" car for the Chicago City Railway, 1912 ▲

Winnipeg Electric 244

The Winnipeg Electric Railway Company decided as far back as 1904 to build its own cars, using a carpentry department set up in its Fort Rouge shops. Both cars #686 (1914-1954) and #244, ex-#214 (1907-1955) were built there and reflect the Winnipeg philosophy of heavy, high-riding vehicles to cope with deep winter snows.

The PAYE concept had been adopted between receipt of the two orders, but all were subsequently rebuilt for one-man operation.

Photo: Richard R. Andrews

33

Chicago North Shore & Milwaukee Railway 500

▲ Although best known for its high speed interurban services, North Shore Line had its roots in streetcar operations in Waukegan, Illinois, and later in Milwaukee, Wisconsin. Car #500, shown here on Genesee Street, Waukegan, about 1946, was one of a lot of ten, a custom design of 1909 by St. Louis Car Company. These were about as large as any city car (not counting articulateds) and this later made quite a contrast when a #500-class mixed between birney car trips. It was 50 ft. long and weighed 58,000 lbs.

Photo: by Art Stitzel, from Wm. E. Robertson collection

Connecticut Company 1584

Rural and urban transit service in New England was predominantly given with streetcar type equipment, with low speed operation on side- ▶▲ of-the-road trackage. Lines throughout the small state of Connecticut were mostly under the aegis of the Connecticut Company, which in turn

was organized by the New York New Haven & Hartford Railroad to control local transportation there. Many of its cars, like #1584 shown here on the M line in New Haven about 1940, were built by Wason Manufacturing Company (1845-1931) at Springfield, Massachusetts. Wason came under Brill control in the early 1900's.

Photo: Francis J. Goldsmith

Chicago Transit Authority 5769

In the electric railway industry the force of the personality of one person has repeatedly resulted in specialized car designs. Often these ▶▶ were purchased in large quantities, but only for the home property or other sister systems. An example is the "Nearside" type of Philadelphia, Buffalo and Chicago, a concept pursued by Thomas E. Mitten during his tenure as an executive of these lines. In this 1948 photo one of Chicago's so-called "muzzleloaders" is seen around 105th on Cottage Grove, where open trackage ran parallel to Illinois Central Railroad main line and electrified suburban tracks.

Photo: Eugene Van Dusen

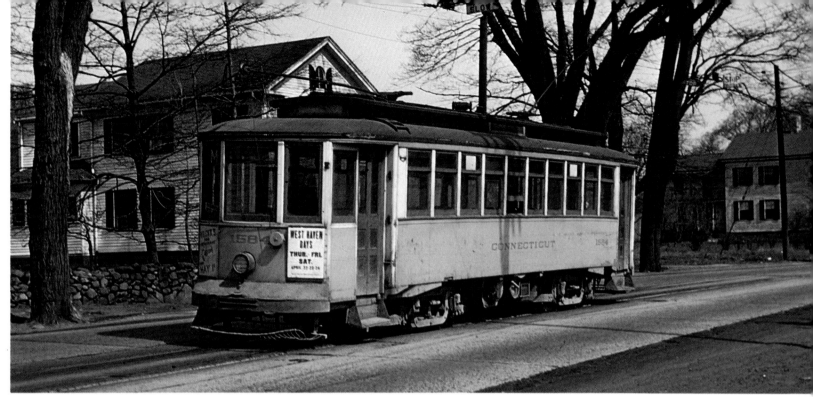

Omaha & Council Bluffs Street Railway 935

◄   Another of those companies that built its own cars, Omaha turned out #935 in 1913. Showing some St. Louis Car influence, it was recorded in its final days in this 1950 photo.
Photo: Eugene Van Dusen

International Railway 6194

▼   Tom Mitten's "Nearside" car concept was employed on a big scale in Buffalo, New York, in this 1912 product of The G. C. Kuhlman Car Co. of Cleveland, Ohio. The photo dates to 1950.
Photo: Eugene Van Dusen

THE CONTROLLER

Perhaps no other streetcar component is more fascinating to the technically interested than the controller. Used continuously by the driver to power, and in many places also to brake the car, the technique of its use could be freely observed almost everywhere. Except in Britain, where no-one was allowed on the front platform, and in Russia, where that pleasure was reserved to the staff and police.

The name of the controller maker, usually cast into the cover plate or stamped into the sheet metal case cover, was as well known or better than that of the car body builder. Thus, there were Union (Thomson-Houston) cars in numerous German towns, Westinghouse cars in Kharkov, Ganz cars in Dnepropetrovsk, and Siemens, AEC and GE cars all over the world.

The first all-round, truly streetcar controller, which provided the fundamental configuration and set the developmental pattern for the next 40 years was the one evolved by Frank J. Sprague for his Richmond, Virginia, cars of 1887. Its basic design was adopted by the industry within the next few years, together with the streetcar shaped by Sprague along the lines the world knows even today.

Sprague's 7½ hp axle-hung, double-reduction motor bore a close resemblance to the Edison dynamos of the time and since Sprague desired to achieve a control system with the least losses, he opted for field control. With this in mind, each of the rather long field magnets was fitted with three coils, those of the two poles being connected permanently in pairs which were connected in series or parallel by a simple drum controller.

This controller consisted of an impregnated wooden drum with screwed-on contact segments. The contact fingers were carried by an insulated board at the back of the controller housing. The fireproof barriers, called arc deflectors, inserted horizontally between the fingers and segments to prevent arcs striking adjacent fingers, came later.

The Richmond controller had seven notches forward and seven reverse, with the OFF position at six o'clock. Turning the handle one way to twelve o'clock accelerated the car to full forward. Turning the other way did the same in reverse. The motors remained in parallel throughout, the individual steps being:

1 — Three sets of magnets in series
2 — Two sets in series, one bridged
3 — Two sets in series, one disconnected
4 — One set in series with two in parallel
5 — Two sets in parallel, one disconnected
6 — Two sets in parallel, one bridged
7 — All three sets in parallel

Addition of a resistance in this circuit resulted in an additional notch, which, followed by the above sequence brought the total number of forward notches to eight. In this case OFF was at twelve o'clock and the crank was moved clockwise to the eighth notch at eight o'clock. Two dynamic brake (short circuit) notches were provided to the left of OFF, with the resistance and all field coil pairs in series on the first and the resistance cut out on the second. The latter was followed by one reverse notch which could be switched in after lifting a hinged stop that otherwise prevented access to this point. This was introduced to prevent easy use, particularly with the car still in motion, since this could cause a "catastrophe" as the disconnection of the brake circuit caused a bad arc which would inevitably short the network. Drivers were well aware of this and took great care in turning down power to avoid severe controller damage. The motor cut-out switch, separate from the controller, was located near the center of the car.

When Thomson-Houston took up the manufacture of streetcar equipment in 1888, it developed the rheostatic controller. This consisted of a semi-circular assembly of 43 cast iron contacts, with resistance elements accommodated between these. This was grouped around a centrally-located blow-out coil invented by Professor Elihu Thomson. The rheostat was mounted under a seat close to the motors and was operated with the aid of steel cables from a notchless controller handle and shaft on the driver's platform. If two motors were used, they were connected in parallel.

To begin with, Siemens adhered to a single motor driving both axles through chains running in oil-filled casings. Their control was by a simple circular switch with four power notches in either direction. An additional switch selected POWER, OFF or BRAKE, the latter permitting two-step motor reversal.

Up to this time, cars with two motors had them connected permanently in parallel. The potential benefits to be secured by the use of series-parallel control had already been elucidated in 1881 in British Patent Specification No. 2989 granted to Dr. Edward Hopkinson (1849-1898), one of the foremost electrical engineers of the time. In his claim he stated:

> "In order to economically vary the speed of a tramcar, tram engine or other vehicle driven by electricity, two dynamo electric machines may be used on the car, engine or vehicle, and when high speed is desired, these are arranged in parallel circuit; when a low speed and greater tractive force is required, they are arranged in series." By this means, less power is dissipated during control operation.

The advantages of series-parallel control were quickly appreciated and the system was universally adopted with the appearance of the K-type controllers designed by Messrs. Potter and Parshall of the newly formed General Electric Company. This was the classic prototype of all successful streetcar controllers which, with slight variations, were produced by the world's manufacturers well into the 1930's.

The K controller "had it all," including an effective magnetic blow-out and arc deflectors, series-parallel control with three step shunt transition from series to parallel motor connection, convenient motor cutout, and, if required, dynamic braking notches. In its K-2 form, with 5 S + 4 P notches, it swept all before it. About 1898 field shunting steps were added as the 6th and 11th notches, thus providing two running speeds at full series and also at full parallel. The method adopted at the time was to connect a resistance in parallel with the field winding, but this led to unsatisfactory motor performance until a few years later, when commutating poles overcame these difficulties.

Once again, many of the European manufacturers had to follow suit. However, the preference for dynamic braking as the "second independent brake" mandated by regulatory authorities resulted in addition of six or seven brake notches. These were located between six and 10:30 o'clock on the control quadrant, the remainder of the circle being used by nine to eleven power notches and OFF.

True to form, Siemens went their own way again, coming up about 1895 with a two-handle camshaft controller. The right "steering" handle made the basic motor connections, while the left hand "resistance" handle provided 0, 4, 6 or 8 ohms of series resistance. The motorman, with his right hand on the handbrake, started with his left hand moving the "steering" handle counterclockwise from OFF to SERIES, then, still with his left, moved the "resistance" handle clockwise through its steps to zero resistance. Next, his left hand went back to the "steering" handle and moved it from SERIES to PARALLEL. The first bit of this movement released a spring to snap the "resistance" handle back to insert the full resistor. There was no transition, nor any magnetic blow-out to suppress the arcs.

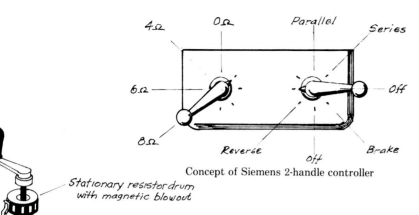

Concept of Siemens 2-handle controller

Stationary resistor drum
with magnetic blowout

Rotating resistor switching arm

Rotating commutating arm
(fingers not shown)

Simplified concept of Siemens 1-handle controller

Siemens' concept replaced the conventional drum with individual camshaft-operated contactors, the stationary contact being of copper and the moveable one fitted with a carbon block. This pairing was chosen to be sure that any nonconductive copper oxide formed by arcing would be reduced to copper. This type of controller was used on cars supplied to Berlin, Dresden and Basel. For the latter the resistance notches were calculated to make available constant speeds down the 1:13.5, 1:16.5 and 1:19 inclines encountered there.

However, before long Siemens changed to a more conventional layout, with 5 S + 4 P + 6 B notches. This controller incorporated a large diameter cylinder carrying contact strips for changing from series to parallel. Resistance cutout contacts were grouped on a stationary cylindrical frame around a blow-out coil above the drum and immediately below the top cover with switching being done by an arm moving in an arc with the main drum.

When removed from the controller for overhaul, the numerous wires leading to the blow-out coil and the resistor elements gave this controller the popular nickname "Lockenkopffahrschalter" ("Curly-headed-controller"). This device was known for its somewhat heavy operation and jerky transition, especially when accelerating on upgrades. Just to be different it seems, the OFF position was mostly at 7:30 o'clock, full PARALLEL was reached clockwise at 3 o'clock and the brake notches were reached counterclockwise between 7:30 and 3 o'clock. In some other cases, there was power counterclockwise from 7:30 to 12 and braking clockwise in the remaining sector from 7:30 to 12.

It is interesting to note that once the relevant patents ran out or licensing agreements were reached, Siemens controller design became similar to the pattern of the K-2s.

J. L. K.

Van DePoele power package of 1888 Pullman car for Dayton, Ohio, had control ▶ box directly on top of the single motor on the front platform. See also text, page 83.

CERA

38

Photo: Pullman, from
G. Krambles collection

Sacramento City Lines 38

"California" type cars were still being produced in 1914: witness this product of St. Louis' American Car Company. Not only was its architecture a decade behind the times, but so was its all-wood construction. Picture date to October 1944.

Photo: by A. R. Alter, from Bill Billings collection

Chicago Surface Lines 1818

Chicago Railways was one of the operators that successfully built its own streetcars, turning out a hundred of this home-grown design in its West Shops during 1913. An additional fifty each were built by the American and Southern car companies. The design introduced bulkhead changes which added a few seats and was also innovative for the use of field control motors. Weighing 36,000 lbs. complete, this car had to negotiate reliably the 11½% tunnel grades with one of its two motors cut out. Shown in service on the Harrison Street line during 1947.

Photo: Thomas A. Lesh

Dallas Railway & Terminal Company 433

A distinctive design of streetcar was developed by the Stone & Webster Management Association for use on its lines spread coast-to-coast, east-to-west and north-to-south. Roof design included a flat arch over the platforms and a ▲ deeper, shorter radius arch over the remainder. This combination was thought to form an air scoop to assist ventilation, earning the nickname "turtle-back." Dallas' #433 is seen here in 1948 headed toward downtown at Monroe Junction, southwest of the central area. This is the point where the Texas Electric interurban shops were located (background) and its route to Corsicana diverged from that to Waco.

Photo: Eugene Van Dusen

Salt Lake City Lines 713

A "standard" design was developed for Salt Lake City and the first lot of 24 were delivered to Utah Light & Railway, as it was then known, by the American Car Company in 1914. The young city had been laid out with unusu- ► ally wide streets and so it was easy to operate rather large cars, like these 50-footers. Steel was used extensively for the bottom and side construction. The 1944 view shows the type after conversion for one-man operation.

Photo: by Art Alter, from Bill Billings collection

Compania Electrica de Tampico 25

Once managed by Ebasco Services of New York, this Mexican line operated twelve miles of standard gage 600 volt DC car line. Its early cars were a lot of 20 built by Brill to a semi-convertible design updated to the 1914 shop date. ►► Such a car was #25, shown here in 1959. Last cars to run here included former Kansas City PCC's.

Photo: William C. Janssen

City of Shaker Heights, Department of Transportation 25
  Better known as Shaker Heights Rapid Transit, this municipal operation was successor to the Cleveland Inter-urban Railroad and predecessor to today's Greater Cleveland Regional Transit Authority. Its operations began in ▲ 1920, but early cars, like the ones shown here on the Green Road loop in 1954, had been built by Kuhlman in 1914 and were obtained for the Cleveland Railway. They were single-end center-door cars fitted with Westinghouse "cabinet" multiple-unit control.

Photo: by H. S. Babcock, from R. R. Andrews collection

Third Avenue Railway System 324
  This New York City system had an exceptionally capable mechanical department. Witness this 1949 photo of car #324, recorded to have been built 1898 by American Car Company and rebuilt 1932 in the company shops. It's hard ▶ to see what, if anything was saved! TARS certainly undertook a mammoth rebuilding program including many innovative improvements of their own design.

Photo: Charles V. Hess

Boston Elevated Railway 4407
  Boston's #4400s were built as #7000s for the Eastern Massachusetts Street Railway in 1927 and were acquired still in like-new condition in 1936. A fine example of the light weight steel safety car of its period, this type had four ▶▶ GE265 (35 hp) motors, Brill 177-E1-X trucks and K35 KK platform controllers. These cars remained in service until 1950.

42

Photo: O. R. Cummings

44

Baltimore Transit Company 5660

▲ Baltimore's extensive streetcar system was a persistent user of Brill's semi-convertible design, with many hundred such cars, some, like 5660 shown here in action in 1951, built as recently as 1917. By then, both their construction details and architecture were becoming outdated, but conservative management seemed well pleased with their proven, dependable design.

Photo: Eugene Van Dusen

Kansas City Public Service 1234

◀ This was one of the order of 50 substantial steel single-enders built by American Car Company in 1915 for the Metropolitan Street Railway, predecessor of Kansas City Public Service. Body corner posts were especially reinforced to resist racking of the roof on the city's steep grades. Photo taken at Waldo Station, 75th and Wornall Streets in 1942.

Photo: by H. S. Babcock, from R. R. Andrews collection

Eastern Massachusetts Street Railway 4389

◀◀ The semi-convertible concept carried over into steel cars like Eastern Massachusetts Street Railway's #4389, built in 1917 by Laconia (New Hampshire) Car Company for Eastern Mass.' predecessor, the Bay State Street Railway. Powered with 4-GE247 motors with PC remote control, 39 like this were acquired when the Chelsea Division of EM was taken into Boston Elevated in 1936.

Photo: Robert C. Gerstley

45

Chicago & West Towns 103

This small system operated over 70 miles of track in western suburbs of Chicago. All of its 88 cars were built by Cummings Car & Coach (or its predecessor, McGuire-Cummings) of Paris, Illinois. Car 103 is shown in October 1941, ▲ southbound on the longest piece of single track in the system, the half-mile on 19th Avenue in Maywood.

Photo: Charles A. Brown

Pittsburgh Railways 4383

Pittsburgh in the 1910s-1920s was one of those cities with very individualistic ideas about car design. Under the leadership of P. N. Jones, its unique angular car bodies, low floor and special motor/control design were featured. ▶ The scene shows local city operation in Washington, Pennsylvania, (about 25 miles south-southwest of Pittsburgh) as it looked late in 1952. This service and the interurban to Pittsburgh were cut a few months later.

Photo: by G. E. Lloyd, from E. Van Dusen collection

Cooperative Transit Company 1

The former Wheeling Traction Company, Cooperative operated 75 cars over about 46 miles of 62½" gage city/ suburban lines. Car #1 was a product of the Jewett Car Company in 1917, when that Newark (Ohio) plant was ▶▶ nearing its end. The photo was taken on an October 1941 fan trip, as witness the destination plate above the headlight.

Photo: W. E. Schriber

Piedmont & Northern Railway 2

In many ways Piedmont & Northern was a trunk line railroad, but it included a few interurban passenger trains and, surprisingly, a one-car local service in the town of Gastonia, North Carolina. This 1941 photo, taken at Groves Mill stop, shows one of the last cars built by John Stephenson plant of Brill. Original owner is thought to have been the nearby Salisbury & Spencer Railway, but the car had been refitted to operate from P & N 's 1500 v trolley.

Photo: Norton D. Clark

Public Service Coordinated Transport 2681
    Newark, New Jersey, initiated a subway utilizing the former alignment of the Morris Canal in 1935. Although better known today for its well-maintained PCC cars, it began with the standard car shown here, a 1917 product of the company's own shops. Again one finds a design reflecting the distinctive ideas of a strong local management.

Photo: Eugene Van Dusen

D.C. Transit System, Inc. 766

    General George McClelland's statue guards Connecticut Avenue at California Avenue in this 1961 glimpse of #766 of the Washington system. The 1918 product of Brill's Kuhlman plant, #766 was last of its kind on a system that used basically PCC-type equipment. Note the visual cleanliness resulting from the use of understreet conduit-enclosed power rails, an operating problem no less!

Photo: Raymond De Groote

Metropolitan Transit Authority 6108

    One more example of a property that developed its own idiosyncrasies in car design was Boston, where the type CEM (and its trailer predecessor) came aboard in the period 1915-1920. The 6100s and 6200s were fitted for multiple-unit train operation, but not the 6300s (not of course the trailer 7000s). Photographed on Beacon Street around 1948.

Photo: Robert C. Gerstley

Cincinnati Street Railway 2258-2506-1114

Three generations of streetcar technology are posed in this scene of about 1948: #2258, Cincinnati Car Company product of 1919; #2506, one of the 1923 curved-side cars also built by Cincinnati; and #1114, a St. Louis-built PCC of 1940.

Photo: Eugene Van Dusen

Lehigh Valley Transit Co. 922

Brill built series #900-923 for LVT in 1918. Originally a center-entrance type with multiple-unit control, they were rebuilt in LVT's shops to eliminate center doors and install double-stream front doors. Photographed within a few weeks of the 1953 demise of streetcars in the vicinity of Allentown, Pennsylvania.

Photo: J. Wallace Higgins

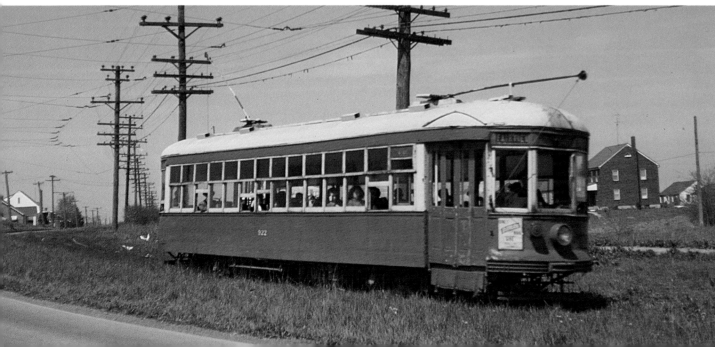

52

Milwaukee & Suburban Transport Company 894

Its competent technical staff kept the physical plant of "TM" (as Milwaukee's transit system was best known) at the leading edge of the industry. Rolling stock chief John H. Lucas, who began his career at Pullman, oversaw development of passenger oriented designs for its thousand car fleet. St. Louis built 10 of the #800-type in 1918-1919. Here is #894 at the switches into private right-of-way on Wells at 52nd Street in 1957.

Photo: Thomas H. Desnoyers

Bangor Railway & Electric Company 44

The "Bosen-Birney" car (Birney for short, no pun intended) developed in 1916 with high hopes that it would be the salvation of the street railway business, became ubiquitous in dozens of small American cities. This one, built by American Car Company in 1919, operated over a 67 track-mile system at Bangor, Maine. Photo taken in 1945.

Photo: R. L. Day

53

Sacramento Northern Railway 62

Here's a "Bosen-Birney" one may ride today at the California Railway Museum at Rio Vista. It had been built by American Car Company in 1920. Its original owner, the San Diego Electric Railway, phased out its birneys after only a few years and about 1923 its #301 became Sacramento Northern #62. It worked local lines in Sacramento, Marysville and Chico, where it made the final day of streetcar service, December 15, 1947. It was saved from the torch by the Bay Area Electric Railway Association and is shown in this 1951 view at San Francisco's East Bay Terminal, on a railfan trip that set a prophetic precedent for Muni's popular historic trolley service of the 1980s.

Photo: LeRoy O. King, Jr.

THE "BOSEN-BIRNEY" SINGLE-TRUCK ONE-MAN SAFETY CAR

During the years preceding World War I some U.S. street railways began to suffer from a pronounced reduction in the rate of traffic growth. In some cases, initially confined to smaller properties, there was actually a decline which accumulated by the end of the conflict to a loss of up to 50% of passengers who began riding in their own automobiles.

At first this disturbing development was countered by some undertakings acquiring new cars along the lines evolved for service in the big cities, i.e., rather large double-truck units. By their very nature, such big cars ended up running at correspondingly greater intervals, even though it was in the small towns that people could, likely as not, walk to their destination rather than wait 15-30 minutes for the next streetcar. What was needed was better, but not necessarily *larger* cars, and with them maybe there was a way to have "a car always in sight."

If large double-truck cars could not meet this demand standard for better service, could another design provide more frequent and faster cars at lower costs, especially those of wages and power? An optimal market target for the time seemed to be to have seven to twenty passengers per car for about fifteen hours of each day, and to have capacity to absorb at least 40 per car in rush hours.

Some of these emerging requirements were met by the twelve one-man single-truck prepayment cars put into service in 1912 at Lockport, New York, by the Mitten managed International Railway Company. Not surprisingly patterned after the Mitten "Nearside" Buffalo car, these 30' long, 22,620 lb. cars accommodated 36 seated and 24 standing passengers. Entrance/exit was via manually-operated folding doors at the front. The car body weighed 9,500 lbs., the truck 5,220 lbs., electrical equipment 6,700 lbs., and air brakes 1,200 lbs. There were no special safety devices as compared to conventional cars of the time. Conditions were ripe for a significant technological breakthrough in car design.

Two outstanding men almost simultaneously came up with identical solutions. They were, "in order of appearance," J. M. Bosenbury, the innovative Superintendent Motive Power & Equipment of the Illinois Traction System, with headquarters at Peoria, Illinois, and C. O. Birney, Superintendent of Car Construction, Stone & Webster Engineering Corporation, a part of the nationwide utility investment and operating organization of like name, with headquarters at Boston.

Illinois Traction operated about 750 streetcars over 330 miles of track in some nineteen small towns and cities in Illinois, Iowa, Kansas, Missouri and Nebraska in addition to its well-known 550-mile interurban system in Illinois. Stone & Webster managed 26 street railways embracing 1,300 cars and about 1,000 miles of track stretching from Boston to Seattle to Houston.

While the idea of a one-man streetcar was anything but new, that of a light weight "safety" car was. Bosenbury and Birney independently set out to evolve such designs, aided by an industry keenly interested in any product which might arrest its decline. The solutions produced by the two men were practically identical.

Bosenbury, aided by St. Louis Car Company, developed a 22'-4" long by 7'-8" single-end car mounted on a truck having 8' wheelbase and 24" wheels permitting a floor height of only 27". Sample car 400 emerging in January 1916, weighed only 10,000 lbs. while offering 30 seats. Entrance/exit was via a 32" wide folding front door coupled to a fold-down step. There was an emergency door centered on the rear end; it was held by a lock that had a combined pneumatic and manual control. The pneumatic feature could be actuated either by an emergency brake application or by pulling a cord extended through the car. The follow-up release of the manual lock permitted the outward-hinged door to be opened with the rearmost hinged seat swinging outward and downward to form an exit step!

Contrary to reducing weight at no sacrifice in stamina, this first design proved flimsy and a bit small. The succeeding model was beefed up to 29'-7½" long and offered 41 seats. The weight of 9,050 lbs. for body, 4,200 lbs. for truck, 2,000 lbs. for electrical and 750 lbs. for air brake totalled to 16,000 lbs.

This substantially improved, well-engineered, sturdy car should have secured Bosenbury's claim to paternity of the "safety" car. But Illinois Traction's street railways were comparatively modest. ITS could award no big car orders and got little publicity for its city lines. To cap it all, "Bosy" (to his friends) had a name a shade too long for catchy reference.

Practically concurrent with the Illinois work, Birney completed designs for a 10,000 lb. single-truck car for 29 seated passengers. Two sample cars were completed early in 1916 at the American Car Company plant only a few miles away from the rival plant working on the Bosenbury sample. Birney's car was 22'-10" long by 7'-6" wide. Its body weighed in at 4,050 lbs. The 8' wheelbase truck with 24" diameter wheels weighed 3,000 lbs. Electrical parts weighed 2,333 lbs. and the air brakes, 617 lbs.

Birney's car was almost identical to Bosenbury's, down to the rear emergency door and the spartan interior finish with little thermal and sound insulation. The somewhat primitive truck incorporated quarter-elliptic and spiral springs, the latter being compressed home at about two-thirds seated load. An additional coil spring provided at the center of each side frame carried about a quarter of the rather minimal body structure. This led to low frequency body pitching and this, in turn, resulted in increased amplitude of oscillation scarcely conducive to good riding, particularly on the deteriorating track in many towns.

Power was furnished by two Westinghouse Electric "Efficiency" (WEE) #505 motors rated 17.5 hp each and weighing only 890 lbs. The K-10 controller, weighed 135 lbs. and had 5 S + 4 P steps.

Heart of the "safety" car was a pneumatic system devised jointly by Bosenbury with the Westinghouse Air Brake Company and used since 1913 on some older Illinois Traction stock resembling single-truck Nearside cars. This novel air equipment combined brake, sanding and door control with a hinged "dead man" controller handle. Unless this handle (or a foot by-pass pedal) was held depressed, the plunger of a small air cylinder would pop out to trip the main circuit breaker, cutting off traction power. Simultaneously a relay valve would cause an emergency brake application, feed air to the track sanders, and, remove air pressure from the closing side of the door and step engines so that both could be opened by hand. The M-28 brake valve developed for the safety car included door control, but it required a full service brake application to open the doors, since the door-open position was to the right of service on a quadrant that went (L to R): Release and door close, service, door open, and, emergency (same effect as handle-up). This often resulted in rough "stone-wall" stops.

After development tests on the Illinois cars, the equipment was marketed by a new Westinghouse subsidiary, Safety Car Devices Company, headquartered in St. Louis.

Reflecting on the record to this point, our contemporary traction historian, Professor Harold E. Cox, states:

> "Credit for the finalization of the concept of the single-truck one-man light-weight safety car, therefore, must go to Bosenbury rather than Birney." In all fairness, may we call it the "Bosen-Birney?"

The reasons for the common reference to Birney in part include the substantial commitment made by Stone & Webster to the introduction of the safety car. By 1917 S & W had on order some 250 such cars, by now in single-end version seating 32 and weighing 13,000 lbs., and in double-end version seating 35 and weighing 13,500 lbs. Standard power had moved up to two 25 hp motors; a few hill-climbers even had 35 hp machines!

In the next few years the design was gradually enhanced as experience exposed features that failed to stand up in service or were unacceptable to riders. By 1918, Birney could say:

"While I was in Tampa recently, riding over the lines on one of their new 'Safety cars' with the Mayor, a number of councilmen and railway officials, I was impressed more than ever with the remarkable riding qualities of the Brill truck. I believe it is the best single-truck that has ever been built. The railway and city officials said that the car rode as smoothly and steadily as any double-truck car they ever had on the lines . . . "

. . . which could mean all things to all men!

Further changes came by 1921, notably in strengthened construction, easier riding trucks, larger wheels to improve clearance over winter's snows, improved brake rigging, more comfortable seats, reduced step height, better lighting, side lining and double flooring, storm sash, ventilators that could be closed if required, and better heating. Car weights crept up to 16,000 lbs. One must remember that the original S & W installations were in southern and Puget Sound cities with mild climates, and that greater passenger capacity also had become desirable.

To safeguard the operator from passing street traffic when a car was at a terminal changing ends, most safety cars were provided with two trolley poles. It was necessary only for the operator to raise one and lower the other, not to "walk" the pole around the car as in many older single-truckers. It did happen once in a while that a car would be started with *both* poles up, followed by delay and damage to poles and overhead. To avoid this, some cars were wired so that motor current was fed via the lead pole and its trolley hook. Lights and compressor would be fed from the line connecting the two poles, however, so as not to leave a dark car standing out in traffic while changing ends.

The rapid adoption on one-man four-wheel "safety" cars was truly remarkable. In the fall of 1916 some 12-15 cars were placed in service by Stone & Webster at Fort Worth, Texas; Bellingham and Everett, Washington. Within six months they were convinced that a worthy new principle of operation had been discovered. The manufacturers involved agreed and proceeded to sponsor the idea for all it was worth. Some 187 such cars were built in 1916, 280 in 1917, 1,620 in 1919, and a peak of 1,699 in 1920, a year that saw double-stream doors employed on a wide scale. Thereafter requirements declined to 565 in 1921 and faded after 1923, with some 6,000 in all having been delivered.

Initially, such cars cost $3,500-$4,000 each. By the end of 1918, they ran $5,400; $6,000 in 1920, and $7,000 in 1921, settling back to about $6,000 thereafter. Stone & Webster acquired 247 for their Virginia lines, 104 for Tampa, 86 for Fort Worth, 65 for Houston, 63 for Seattle, 59 for Tacoma, 45 for Galveston and 40 for El Paso. Other extensive users included the Eastern Massachusetts Street Railway with 251, Detroit with 250, Brooklyn 212; Public Service Company of New Jersey, 200; and the Connecticut Company, 167. But their popularity faded fast, and by 1932 only about 200 were left in the entire country.

One of the most workmanlike single-truck safety cars was #2006 of Chicago Surface Lines, weighing a total of 16,375 lbs. divided into a 7,000 lb. body, 2,800 lbs. of motors, 4,690 lb. truck, 1,585 lbs. of brakes, and 270 lbs. of miscellany. It was crafted in CSL's own shops and included many refinements. Yet CSL settled for only one car of that design, plus ten more typical Birneys, out of its 3,600 car fleet!

Birney cars were also acquired, mostly from Brill, for service in Canada, Argentina, Brazil, Columbia, Mexico and New Zealand. Three were used as trailers at Arnhem, Holland. A small fleet ran in Bendigo, Australia, until 1972.

For a short while the Birney safety car could do no wrong and in 1920 one could read that: "The safety car has been such a tremendous success that no urban electric railway in North America can afford to neglect its possibilities; its use will be very rapidly extended until the bulk of all-day runs, of basic schedules, in every city will be handled with these cars." Also, "we can confidently say that the safety car will, on the average, produce sufficiently more net income to pay for itself in less than two years. To many railways, its use to the maximum extent, will spell all the difference between prosperity and bankruptcy."

However, such contentment was short-lived, even though the operating expenses of many undertakings were stated to have been reduced some 43% on the average. Collisions with other vehicles became more frequent and the damage done to safety cars was greater than to the older heavy cars. The front entrance and exit encouraged passengers riding only a short distance to remain at the front. This not only slowed all boarding and alighting, but on such light cars it unloaded the rear wheels, sometimes enough to cause violent spinning when starting. Gear noise was insufficiently damped by the light (and not altogether tight) gear cases.

Nor could the four-wheelers compete with double-truck cars in riding quality, for the simple, but sometimes overlooked fact that the former cannot provide the shock reducing properties of the latter. When running over vertical irregularities such as rail joints or rough track, the impacts encountered by the wheels of a single-truck car are transmitted via the suspension to the car body, whereas the lever action of the truck frame of a double-truck car would, at the very least, halve their intensity. The lateral (horizontal) displacements encountered are similarly diminished by the geometry of double trucks.

As an example, in the case of a standard gage four-wheeler with 8' wheelbase running down straight track, and particularly when entering a curve without benefit of a transition, the front will swing about a vertical axis 12" to the rear of the rear wheelset. The lateral forces resulting are mitigated only by the swing links or similar devices provided between the truck and the body frame. With a double-truck car having 6' wheelbase trucks, these would be displaced about a vertical axis some 16" back of each *truck* rear wheelset and here too the forces transmitted to the car body would be halved by the truck frame levering action. Thus whatever claims are made favorable to single-truck vehicles, their riding qualities will never be as good as those of double-truck ones, an especially important consideration when it came to poorly maintained track endemic to financially starved small town systems.

This, together with low performance (20 mph max. speed) available from small motors, uncomfortable seats and austere interior, was scarcely helpful to managements in marketing Birney service against fast-growing auto competition. Playful student passengers, observing the bobbing cars, learned to bounce them by jumping up and down at the natural pitching frequency to an extent causing derailment. In other cases, well-meant soft suspensions combined with crush loads to force the floor down on the wheel flanges, causing complaints that the floor was "getting too hot for standing!" In only a couple of inches of snow, cars were reported to be "just sitting there and howling like hell!" Introduction of Peter Witt cars in Detroit even led to the unpopular Birneys being nicknamed "Half-Witts."

The single-truck safety car had an intense influence, but not a lasting one, on the outlook of street railway operators. Even when it failed, many of its features were transferred to double-truck designs. Fundamentally these resembled the earlier Nearside solution modified to become a one-man car with deadman control handle, brakedoor interlock and the other related safety features. For urban service, the double-truck Birney design was unable to meet increasingly demanding operating requirements. The large cars with their rather small doors and excessive dependence on front doors yielded an interior arrangement that obstructed passenger circulation. Like the last Bourbon kings, their creators learned nothing and forgot nothing.

The "Bosen-Birney" single-truck safety car was conceived as an improvement for low speed, light traffic volume urban passenger travel. The safety features as applied to double-truck versions and more advanced designs found some success in interurban modernization of the 1920s.

J. L. K.

Philadelphia Transportation Company 1

Some of the mighty systems tried the tiny "Bosen-Birneys." One such was at Philadelphia, which did so in a token sort of way, as documented by this 1943 view of its #1 on Route 78, a shuttle line between Darby and Lansdowne in the southwest part of its service area. It was a Brill of 1922 vintage, and of course conformed to the city's 62½″ track gage. There were only five of this type car in the city's fleet of more than 3,000 streetcars.

Photo: Charles A. Brown

Conestoga Transportation Company 240

Alike as most birneys appeared, there were many individual variations, such as this double-door version, a Brill product of 1923, shown on the Duke Street Route at the Pennsylvania Railroad station in Lancaster, Pennsylvania in the 1940s. Another 62½" (Pennsylvania Trolley) gage system, Conestoga had more than 70 cars running over 30 miles of urban and rural trackage.

Photo: James P. Shuman

Virginia Electric & Power Company 1456
  Norfolk had Brill birneys, built in 1926 following the most typical single-door double-end format, but running on 62″ gage track (unlike the same company's standard gage Richmond lines). Norfolk had a relatively extensive system, with more than 400 cars and 108 miles of track at its peak. This photo was taken in 1943.

Photo: Francis J. Goldsmith

59

Home Transit Incorporated

When Indiana Railroad abandoned its interurban line between Seymour and Louisville, part of the old Interstate Public Service Company's route that extended into Indianapolis and once ran parlor-diner and sleeping cars between Indianapolis and Louisville, a local company was formed to run the city lines in New Albany, Indiana, on the north side of the Ohio River opposite Louisville, Kentucky. The new owner was called Home Transit and maintained service using the existing cars. Car #95 shown here was originally #5078 of Boston's Eastern Massachusetts Street Railway, Brill-built and acquired by Interstate Public Service in 1927, along with three others, at a cost of $2,925 each. Stark Electric of Canton, Ohio, had bought three of the same lot a few weeks earlier.

Photo: George G. McKinley

Johnstown Traction Company 311
 The safety car concept and many of the single-truck birney body structural characteristics were adapted to double-truck cars by most of the carbuilders then operating. This is one built in 1922 by the Wason Car Company of Springfield, Massachusetts, for the Pennsylvania steel mill of Johnstown. It is shown here on the Moxham bridge in 1960.
Photo: Eugene Van Dusen

St. Petersburg Municipal Railway

Here's an American Car Company version of a double-truck safety car, in a photo of about 1942. This one had double-stream vestibule doors but otherwise closely resembles the Johnstown car shown in the preceding photo. This Florida car was supplied in small lots apparently totalling only nine units. They were 40 ft. long, weighed about 30,000 lbs. and were powered with four 25 hp motors. At the time St. Petersburg had a population of only 25,000 and operated about 50 cars on 35 miles of track. Today the Tampa-St. Petersburg urban area boasts over 1,500,000 people!

Photo: by H. S. Babcock, from R. R. Andrews collection

San Diego Electric Railway 413

 The basic safety car pattern as carried to an apex of technology was exemplified by the fifty #400-series cars which were delivered by the American Car Company to San Diego, mostly in 1924. Having double-stream doors at all four corners, this type originally was fitted with pantographs, multiple-unit control and couplers to permit train service. Two-car trains were common and there were even occasional threes. Photo shows car on one of the Balboa Park viaducts in 1946. These cars were scrapped with the abandonment of car lines in 1946-1947. However, after some 35 years of bus-only service, San Diego is now enjoying a renaissance of electric railway service with the successful San Diego Trolley Inc. between downtown and the International Border at San Ysidro. Yet another route is nearing completion at this writing.

Photo: by A. R. Alter, from Bill Billings collection

63

Louisville Railway 774

The Peter Witt carbody arrangement involved front entrance and center exit, with fare collection as the rider passed a conductor stationed just forward of the center doors. The car shown here was G. C. Kuhlman Car ▲ Company's execution of such a design for the Kentucky metropolis. However, when this photo was taken in 1946, #774 had already gone through the easy conversion to one-man operation.

Photo: Dr. Howard Blackburn

St. Louis Public Service Company

This busy Missouri city was one of those that built many cars in its own shops, developing a specialized design of low-floor Peter Witt type of which #931 was one turned out in 1923. This car weighed about 39,000 lbs. and rode on ►▲ Commonwealth cast steel MCB form trucks with inside hung 35 hp motors. The body architecture was distinguished by unusually deep windows and ends with semi-circular floor plan. Photo about 1949.

Photo: by H. S. Babcock from R. R. Andrews collection

New Orleans Public Service Company 803

New Orleans also had its own style of car. This 1922 Brill was built to a typical Pay-As-You-Enter car floor plan. It's one of the very few car types illustrated in this volume which may be seen in service at this writing, although ►► this photo dates to 1961. While transit was part of the NOPSI corporation its costs and receipts were integrated with those of gas and electric services. This in effect subsidized transit through the utility rates since the 1920s and resulted in a remarkably higher riding habit than in other cities of comparable size.

Photo: Thomas H. Desnoyers

Memphis Street Railway 606

St. Louis Car Company completed a lot of 40 lightweight two-man double-end cars for Memphis on New Year's
▲ Eve of 1923. Controversial at the time was a switch with this order from rattan to wooden slat seats, for claimed
"sanitary" reasons in view of the Jim Crow law of that day! The problem went away when the cars were converted
for single-end operation and upholstered leather seats were installed. Photographed about 1940.

Photo: by H. S. Babcock from R. R. Andrews collection

Sacramento City Lines 62

Extrapolation from the single-truck Birney concept to the design of the American Car Company product of 1920 is
▲◄ clear. It's seen here at the Southern Pacific depot in California's capital city, as it looked in 1944.

Photo: by A. R. Alter, from Bill Billings collection

Home Transit Inc. 253

Cincinnati Car Corporation applied its own ingenuity to the development of lightweight single- and double-truck
◄◄ safety cars. Its "Curved-siders" and arch-bar framed trucks became a legend in their own right. Home Transit (ex-
Indiana, ex-Interstate) #253 is shown in New Albany, Indiana, in 1943.

Photo: George G. McKinley

67

Reading Transit 803

Reading celebrated 1923 as the 175th Anniversary of the founding of this Pennsylvania city by building some #800-series lightweights in its own shops, using frames supplied, some by Brill and others by the local Progress Iron Works. Patterned after Boston's famous "Type 5," car #803 shown here at Mohnton terminal about 1940, was one of these. Brill also supplied two complete #800's, diverting them to Reading from a contemporary Boston order. Reading's track gage was 62½".

Photo: G. W. Gerhart

Philadelphia Transportation Company 5333

In July 1923 Brill began delivery of 576 cars, up to that time the largest single order for electric railway rolling stock. Evolving from the previous "Nearside" design, 385 single-enders were of the Peter Witt plan, 135 were double-end PAYE type, and the balance were various types of work cars. The PAYE cars, of which #533 is shown in this 1957 view, were of lightweight construction. All of the passenger cars rode on Brill's highly successful type 39-E trucks.

Photo: Thomas H. Desnoyers

Columbus & Southern Ohio Electric Company 702

Shown here is #702, built in 1926 by Brill's G. C. Kuhlman plant, one of 23 cars for Columbus, Ohio. They were 45 ft. long, double-end PAYE type. As of 1940, this system operated a total of 107 miles of track, some of it 56½" gage ▲ and the remainder, 62" gage. It had nearly 200 cars then.

Photo: Eugene Van Dusen

Worcester Street Railway 515

There were about 60 cars operating over some 32 miles of track in Worcester, Massachusetts, in 1945 when this photo was taken of cars #515 and #598. Both cars had been built in the 1920s in the local plant of the Osgood Bradley ▶▲ Car Company, later a component of Pullman-Standard.

Photo: R. L. Day

Key System (East Bay Transit) 978

The 95 cars of the #900-class built in 1925 by American Car Company became the Oakland, California area's newest "standard" car. Weighing in at 40,000 lbs., this car was 44'-10" long and had four 40 hp motors. After the ▶▶ demise of East Bay streetcars, one of this type ran out its days as #4011 of Portland's Oregon City interurban. This photo was taken in 1944.

Photo: by A. R. Alter, from Bill Billings collection

70

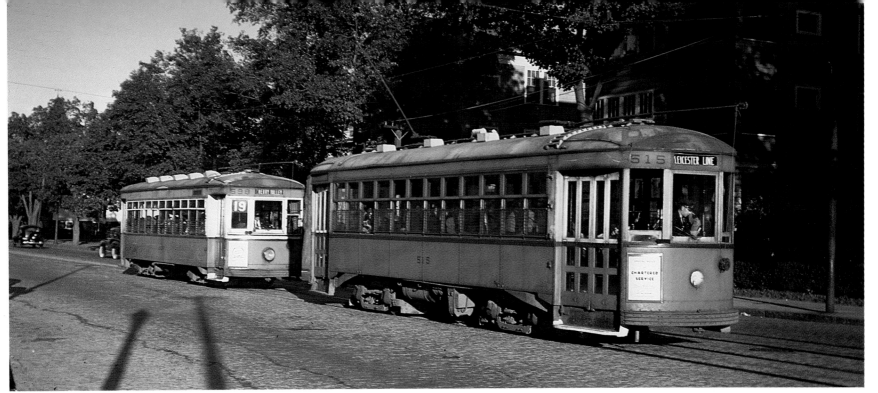

71

United Electric Railways Company 2170

Emerging from an underpass below the Providence, Rhode Island station of the New Haven Railroad is #2170, a product of the Wason Car Company in 1926. One of a lot of 35 cars that rode on Brill 177-E-1 trucks with 27″ wheels, it was 41 ft. long, powered with four 35 hp motors and weighed 35,000 lbs. This photo dates to about 1948.

Photo: Robert C. Gerstley

Virginia Electric & Power Company 209

Acquired in 1941 from the Cincinnati & Lake Erie city operation in Dayton, Ohio, #209 was a peppy 41-footer built in 1927 by the Cincinnati Car Company. Weighing 33,400 lbs., this single-end type rode on Brill 177-E-1X trucks and was powered by four GE-265 motors rated 35 hp. Photo taken in 1948 on the standard gage Richmond system which listed 178 cars and 68 track miles as of 1940.

Photo: James P. Shuman

York Utilities Company 90

The last remaining electric railway in the state of Maine, this shorty was operating only about 2½ miles of track between Sanford (where this photo was taken about 1945) and the railroad station at neighboring Springvale, Maine. This so-called River Street route had started life in 1893 as the Mousam River Railroad and was once the westerly terminal of the Atlantic Shore Line Railway which extended to the Atlantic coast at Cape Porpoise and in a north-south direction between Biddeford and Portsmouth, New Hampshire, with about 95 miles of track. Car #90, along with sister car #88, was acquired second hand from the East Taunton (Massachusetts) Street Railway in 1933. They had been built in 1926 by Wason, were 36 ft. long, rode on Brill 177-EX trucks and were powered with four GE-258 motors. Passenger service ended in 1947 after a spectacular derailment nearly dumped car #90 into the river, too accurately fulfilling the destination proclaimed on its destination sign. Freight service was dieselized in 1949 and ended completely in 1961. Car #88 is preserved at this writing in the Seashore Museum at Kennebunkport, Maine.

Photo: Robert C. Gerstley

SOME THOUGHTS ABOUT CAR BODY DESIGN

As one studies the evolution of cars for street and interurban railways, it is evident that great attention has been devoted to the engineering aspects of trucks, brakes and electrical equipment, as well as to door operating and safety features. Rightly so. However, interior and exterior decor were more likely to catch the imagination of the popular press.

To the fourth estate, the body structure was mostly ignored as something rather dull, if unavoidable; something necessary to house the passengers. Yes, the body should provide a modicum of comfort, although impressively luxurious interiors were offered by some interurbans and even today, by a few rapid transit lines seeking to lure riders with carpeting and upholstered walls. Of course, a car body must have doors and windows and, last but not least, carry a paint scheme to provide some special identity. Some electric car liveries seemed to suggest a fast ship in a moderately stormy sea rather than a rail vehicle running alongside country roads or in city streets.

To the technically minded observer some body design features strike one as rather odd, particularly when the safety of operation is considered. For example, the height of couplers on one property ranged from 30"-36" above rail, while the center of anti-climbers ranged from 42"-44" on the older, heavy cars; from 44"-46" on interurban freight trailers; down to only 30" on the newest high-speed lightweight cars! What this meant in case of a collision was all too often evidenced in carnage during the relatively short life span of the fleet concerned.

Apart from the obvious need to have common coupler and anticlimber heights within all the vehicles in one carrier's fleet, it would seem clearly desirable to have similar agreed standards between all railways likely to pass through each other's territory or to exchange cars for whatever reasons. But when segments of a system have been built independently with differing standards, whose shall be modified to achieve standardization? The main line railroads implemented such standards at an early stage. On rapid transit lines the relevant dimensions were determined by platform and car floor heights. Among interurban lines there was little to restrain early development, and by the time the potential of through working was recognized it was so expensive to change standards that few actually completed the metamorphosis.

As far as streetcars were concerned, consider the Wilmington, Delaware system—which in the 1920s demanded a new design with entrance/exit platforms only 14" above rail—apparently assuming absolution from the possibility of collision with cars of more usual designs, or at least that the attractiveness to customers of the easy first step would be worth any such risks.

How is a car body design developed? The structure must, of course, be able to carry the weight of the passenger load. Passenger weight averages about one ton per 16 people. The total weight of passengers can be calculated from this average by determining the number of seated and standing passengers that could get aboard. The seated capacity is obvious from the floor plan. The number of standees (at an average of 2 sq. ft. per person) is estimated by measuring the floor area free of seats, not including a strip of one foot width in front of seats for passengers' feet.

In addition to this static load, the car body has to withstand dynamic loads due to oscillations and impacts caused by track irregularities. To ensure good riding qualities, the static deflection of axlebox and bolster springs should aim at no less than one inch for every 16 mph speed. With this, the dynamic load will amount to about 15% of the static load, which must be added in determining the structural stresses.

The maximum static load should not cause the car body to deflect by more than 0.1% of the distance between truck centers. Passenger comfort will be influenced by body bending oscillations, the frequency of which is likely to be some 20% higher when resting on the trucks than if ascertained with the aid of oscillators and the body on rigid supports. As measured on some 30 modern European high-speed railway cars ready for service, the frequency of body bending ranges 7-13 hz. Most came within the narrower 8-12 hz range and 10 hz would be a representative value. It is very important for this frequency not to be excited within the operationally important speeds, either due to bouncing/pitching oscillations of a truck frame, or by wheel imbalance or eccentricity.

Truck frame oscillation frequencies, essentially determined by the sprung truck mass and its moment of inertia and the axle box spring stiffness, should be either 1.4 times higher or lower than that of the body bending mode, the choice depending upon the latter, the operational speed and the predominating rail length between joints. The importance of keeping wheel imbalance and eccentricity within strict limits becomes apparent when it is considered that to excite a frequency of 10 hz, a 30" wheel would have to run at 67.3 mph as compared to 56 mph in the case of a 36" wheel. Both of these speeds are within the range of interurban or modern high-performance rapid transit trains.

European railways set strict limits on wheel eccentricity. Those operating at 100 mph or more limit total wheel eccentricity to about 0.01"; if not more than 75 mph, they settle for no more than 0.02". As to imbalance, the corresponding limits aimed for are 0.6-0.7, or even 0.4 lb. ft. for very fast service and 1.8 lb. ft. for fast service. The seriousness with which both eccentricity and imbalance are taken on the railways suggests that this aspect of vehicle performance and upkeep should be considered with due attention in view of the ever increasing speeds of city railways.

Another dynamic force which car bodies must withstand is that of acceleration and braking. With conventional brakes retardation values of 6 ft/sec/sec apply, rising to 8.5 ft/sec/sec when magnetic track brakes are added. Particular attention must be devoted to the kingpin or rods which couple the truck to the underframe, since very substantial forces can be experienced, especially in rough shunting, coupling, derailment or collision. Typically, the kingpin should be able to withstand a force equivalent to three times the truck weight in interurban or high-performance transit cars, as compared to only the truck weight for conventional streetcars.

The maximum centrifugal force encountered in cornering curves is not likely to exceed 6.5 ft/sec/sec. Wind pressure may be reasonably assumed not to exceed 12-15 lb./sq. ft. of body side area. Shock loads to be withstood without permanent distortion on high-performance cars can be as high as 80 tons, as compared to 20 tons for streetcars. At the coupler plane, shock may be 10 tons.

Throughout the early years of electric traction, the design and construction of car bodies was the domain of first-class craftsmen who drew on their own unique experience and creative insight. Backed by large supplies of well-seasoned wood available at the carbuilders' yards, they produced car bodies of considerable resistance and durability as well as pleasant architectural appearance. The evolution toward more economical and accident-resistant, lighter, metal bodies posed more exacting problems. Stress and vibration needed to be quantified, and there were new problems of manufacture and maintenance. Assisted by new metallurgical materials, fire-resistant fabrics and plastics, these were mastered within a relatively short space of time.

As a result, cars now emerge lighter, stronger, and in some ways less demanding for operation and maintenance. On the other hand, styling of bodywork and especially the outer appearance has not always retained a pleasant functional impression, certainly not to an extent commensurate with the effort lavished on this aspect by the professional stylists our industry has employed.

J. L. K.

POWER COLLECTION BY TROLLEY POLE OR BOW

In their logical simplicity two truly remarkable basic inventions made possible the electric street railway: the axle-hung motor and the underrunning trolley wheel. While the axle-hung motor was solely due to Frank J. Sprague (1846-1934), the trolley wheel current collector was invented simultaneously and independently by Sprague and Karel (Charles) Van de Poele (1846-1892), the "Edison belge" who, emigrating in 1869 from Belgium, settled in Detroit, later to found the Van de Poele Electric Light Company in Chicago.

In 1885 Van de Poele demonstrated at the Toronto Industrial Exhibition a car fed by a non-reversing underslung trolley pole, but he did not pursue development of this feature until 1888 when once more non-reversing trolley poles were used with streetcars of his design at Ansonia, Connecticut and Dayton, Ohio.

The main problem of this design was the difficulty in making it stay on the wire. Concurrently, Sprague pursued no less than "two score designs of undercontact trolleys," the first being vertical and telescopic. His bright draftsman, Eugene Pommer, evolved the swivelling trolley pole turning on a roof-mounted tripod and fitted with an insulated retrieving line, the first trolley rope.

Van de Poele, then employed by the Thomson-Houston Company which had absorbed his company, evolved a trolley pole turning on a fairly high vertical standard, the helical tension spring being arranged vertically between this and the inclined trolley pole. This design was first used on July 4, 1888 with the two cars of the Crescent Beach, Massachusetts line, followed in the fall of the same year with the cars of the Eckington & Soldiers Home Road in Washington, D.C. The subsequent amalgamation of the Thomson-Houston Company with Edison General Electric (which, in 1890 absorbed Sprague's company) led to development of the trolley current collector as we know it today.

But it took a long time. In 1906 *Street Railway Journal* stated, "The little trolley wheel probably makes more trouble for the average master mechanic than any other single piece of mechanism in the equipment of the road. While there are a number of excellent wheels on the market, a fortune awaits the man who can invent a trolley wheel which will do the work demanded of it and show a life approaching that of the other wearing parts of the equipment. . . . Wheels which have run 6,000 to 8,000 miles are found frequently, yet the next few wheels of the same lot may develop soft spots or may not be perfectly round, and they go to pieces in a few hundred miles."

Thus with the Dayton-Toledo limiteds attaining 60 mph for long stretches over the 320-mile run, it was common to stop once or twice to change trolley wheels. This meant there had to be plenty of spares; many lines carried complete spare poles on the roof of each car despite starting each day with a fresh wheel, using the slightly worn ones on local cars after each day's runs.

As might be expected, wheel life depends on car speed, electrical load, pressure against the wire, condition of wire and trolley fittings, alignment and other factors. A commonly used 6" diameter wheel had 4½" diameter at its contact surface. It revolved 4,500 rpm at 60 mph, and was made of copper alloyed with tin, lead or zinc. It was expected to last 7,500 miles at 18 lbs. contact pressure, 4,200 miles at 28 lbs., 3,000 miles at 34 lbs., and only 2,500 miles at 45 lbs. Actual performance seems to have pressures ranging 20-40 lbs. and lives correspondingly ranging 5,000-500 miles. However, stated pressures were not reliably maintained and, what with the variable effects of windage, it was possible for the values to be twice the stated ones, causing excessive wear, or if only half, causing frequent dewirement.

Time cures many deficiencies. By 1922 average trolley wheel life mileage was 8,300 in city service and 5,000 in interurban work. For city service, the generally standard wheel was 4½" diameter, 1½" wide, weighed 2 lbs. and could collect up to 400 amp at 40 mph. The true running needed for spark-free operation was tested by running a harp-held wheel against a fast-running belt drive, this not being possible with the slightest out-of-balance.

Taking into account the variation in height of car roof plus trolley wire height ranging from 18 to 22 ft., trolley pole length correspondingly varied between 11'-4" and 14'-0". This also depended on car size and the need for the conductor to see the wheel when rewiring a pole, being at its best when running at an angle of 20°-30°. Poles were usually made from light steel tubing 1" in diameter at the harp end, and 1½"-2" at the butt end. Complete with harp, wheel and, in some cases, rubber insulating sleeves, poles weighed 125 to 200 lbs.

Care had to be used in selecting rope with the strength, flexibility and insulation needed for use on trolleys. Bell cord or emergency cord could not be used for trolley rope as it normally would have a metallic core. Special wax-impregnated cord or in-line insulators were needed to insure safe insulation even with wet ropes on voltages above 750 v.

Reliable trolley operation depended upon good riding qualities, well-lubricated trolley wheel bushings, and trolley bases that swivelled freely but prevented grease and oil being deposited on the roof. Care was needed to adjust the suspension to have a perpendicular car body and to prevent undue swaying. The proper trolley pressure and good alignment of overhead had to be maintained.

It is perhaps astonishing that this surprisingly simple method of current collection has been effectively used for so long and at such high speeds as prevailed on some lines, though it has been generally replaced by the trolley shoe and the pantograph.

Contrary to the use of the trolley pole, many European street railways adopted the bow current collector evolved by the Siemens & Halske Company. In 1899, Louis Magee pointed out in the *Street Railway Journal*, "True to the traditions of a firm which laid the very foundations of the electrical industry half a century ago, [Siemens] refused to stake its reputation on the vagaries of the trolley-wheel and started on the modern phase of its career in street railway work with its broad bow or stirrup contact piece."

The task of developing a suitable current collector was assigned in 1890 to Walter Reichel (1867-1937), subsequently Privy Councilor, Dr. Eng., Dr. Eng. h.c. Professor of Electric Railway Engineering at the Technical University of Berlin, Siemens board member and manager of their Dynamo Works. Reichel suggested the use of a sliding contact, ascertaining the feasibility of this by clamping two wires crosswise in a vise to check their ability to transmit the required current loads. The suggestion caused his department head to comment, "this is an unheard of impudence, but . . . let's try it!"

In 1891, two rectangular, spring-loaded frames were mounted on the roof of the original Lichterfelde car, followed by long bow collectors on a new Siemens-built street railway in Genoa and then, in 1893, on a larger scale with street railways in Hannover and Dresden.

Some 50 years ago the writer visited a number of continental street railways to obtain data on current collector mileage of the bows and pantographs then used. Most of these were self-reversing, but a few were arranged to be turned like trolley poles, although locked in position by a spring-loaded ratchet. Since success depended on the contact strip, we were seeking to evolve one with long life, i.e., least wear, highest conductivity and best non-oxidizing qualities. It was known that the sliding contact was more affected by current density than by speed.

To minimize overhead wear, the contact surface should be softer than the overhead, so for the contact, preference was given to grease-filled aluminum U-sections. These were rigidly secured in the bow frame, the leading edge suffering localized wear causing intense radio interference. This led to use of 2" wide W-shaped sections. The original U-section were made of 94% Al 6% Cu. At a pressure of 10 lbs. they lasted 7,500-8,000 and more miles.

With the metal shortages of WW I, use was made of 2⅜" wide, 36" long, triangular electrolytic carbon collector strips. Running in bows 30° to the overhead, these managed to run up 28,000 miles in Frankfurt and some lasted up to 62,000! Equal success was obtained elsewhere, with 30,000 miles at Halle, 75,000-93,000 at Brandenburg, 62,000 at Stettin and 93,000 at Nurenberg.

The Luebeck street railway developed a triangular "wireless preservation" brass collector strip which ran more than 90,000 miles at a pressure of 10 lbs. In Budapest, where wartime copper shortages resulted in replacing some 80% of the overhead with steel wire, steel collector plates were introduced in 1923 by the technical director of the company, Julius Fischer, Knight of Tovaros. The 39″L x 4″ W plate had two 24″ x ½″ x ¼″ grooves, originally filled with a grease made of tallow, vaseline and oil melted together, later superseded by graphite. Either of these, applied weekly in warm weather and daily in frosty weather, adhered to the wire even when wet. To prevent the formation of minute, glass-hard globules caused by arcing, ¼″ brass strips were rivetted to the leading edges. This increased plate life from 14,000 to 18,500 miles. Similar plates were also used at the time by Leipzig, Dresden, Glasgow, Leeds, Sunderland and others.

In the meantime, a twin-strip aluminum current collector was developed by the Siegmund Bergmann Company which ran up life miles of 37,500 to 50,000 on certain German and Polish street railways. Incidentally, all of the wear data above relates to single-truck cars pulling one or two trailers at speeds seldom more than 25 mph. The usual zig-zag staggering of the contact wire was typically 12″-20″ to each side of center.

It is believed that the earliest application of pantograph to light rail came from Thomson-Houston, who developed one carrying a trolley wheel for use in mines where there was insufficient clearance to turn a trolley pole. In later applications the pantograph became more popular as an alternative to pole or bow collectors, until post WW II and it has now become ubiquitous, practically supplanting all other means of overhead collection.

J. L. K.

Cincinnati Street Railway 115

One hundred cars, #100-199, were built for the local transit system by the Cincinnati Car Company in 1928 to the Peter Witt front-entrance-center-exit layout, but the car was equipped at the factory for alternative use with two-man or one-man crew. Weighing about 33,000 lbs., these cars rode on Cincinnati arch-bar trucks. Designed for about 30 mph speed, about half were later souped up to run better than 40 mph. Shown at the Vine Street carhouse in 1946. The property included 240 miles of 62½″ gage track in 1940.

Photo: Dr. Howard Blackburn

City Lines of West Virginia 808

Imagine the traffic problem of crossing a two-lane interstate bridge over the Ohio River on a single-track streetcar line. This 1946 photo shows just such a link connecting Marietta, Ohio with Williamstown, West Virginia, on a route ▲ extending to Parkersburg. The car was a 1928 product built for the predecessor Monongahela-West Penn Public Service Company, by G. C. Kuhlman, and one of their last dozen carbuilding jobs. It's an upgrade of the safety car design, weighing 33,000 lbs., 45'-3" long, riding Brill 117-E-1 trucks and having four W-1425 motors. Streetcar service here ended in 1947.

Photo: Dr. Howard Blackburn

Street Railway Property, City of Phoenix 507-501

This double-truck safety car built by American Car Company in 1928 was not noticeably different from the basic birney design, except as to length. A lot of 18 were ordered as part of the modernization program implemented by ► ▲ the municipality of Phoenix, Arizona upon its acquisition of a dilapidated system of 16 track-miles from a private owner. These cars weighed about 30,000 lbs. with an overall length of 39'-1" and rode on Brill 177-E trucks.

Photo: by A. R. Alter, from Bill Billings collection

Cleveland Transit System 5005

Ahead of its time, this articulated car set a high productivity standard not fully recognized by the industry for another half century when it was out-shopped from the Kuhlman-Brill plant in 1928. Car #5005, shown here leaving ► ► Cleveland Public Square on East Euclid in 1948, seated 104 and was 88'-2½" long, had six 50 hp motors and type HL control. Street car service ended in the 1950s just about the time that Cleveland's rapid transit line came into operation.

Photo: Eugene Van Dusen

Hamilton Street Railway 540

Canadian streetcar builders followed conservative U.S. designs. Hamilton, Ontario's standard modern car was
▲ series #500-547 built in three orders during 1927-1928 by the local National Steel Car Company. Measuring 40'-11"
overall, they weighed 37,000 lbs. The propulsion package included four Westinghouse 510-A motors and single-end
K-35-XB control. The property was unusually specific in its car assignments for a system of over 100 cars. For example, #501-518 were assigned in the 1930s to the Belt Line, with odd numbers running counterclockwise and even
clockwise, while #521-527 were regulars on Burlington-James South and #530-533 on Westdale. Each line ran its cars
in numerical order! Streetcar service here ended in 1951. Photo taken in 1947.

Photo: A. D. Kerr

Altoona & Logan Valley Railway 74

In 1928-1929, with ridership starting to sled, transit managers sought to hold business by providing better equip-
▲◄ ment. Responding, the Osgood Bradley Company of Worcester, Massachusetts, engineered a distinctly different car
with many innovations in style and technology. For example, there was the deep letterboard and low floor, there
were eight independent brake actuators (one per wheel) instead of conventional brake cylinder and foundation
rigging, variable load control, etc. Sample car #1929 was built and tested in Worcester and was sold to York, Pennsylvania. This led to a production run of five cars for Altoona, ten for Scranton (both in Pennsylvania), and twelve for
New Bedford, Massachusetts. Altoona operated about 59 miles of 63" gage track with ±80 cars. Car #74 is shown
here as it appeared in 1953, a few months before the end of street cars here.

Photo: A. D. Kerr

Brooklyn & Queens Transit Corporation 6014

In 1930 Osgood Bradley Car built half of a series of 100 front-entrance center-exit cars for Brooklyn. These were
◄◄ equipped with turnstiles adjacent to the operator for prepayment of fares. Costing an average of $16,000, they
weighed 37,000 lbs., and rode on Brill 177-E-1 trucks with Westinghouse 510 motors.

For whatever reasons, 80 of the cars were fitted with leather-upholstered, spring-cushion bucket seats, while the
remainder had wooden benches. The Brooklyn network included about 300 miles of track and 1,800 streetcars at the
time.

Photo: Francis J. Goldsmith

81

Queensboro Bridge Railway 605

The "Electromobile" cars Osgood-Bradley had built in 1929 for the Union Street Railway were sold (when New Bedford, Massachusetts closed down its streetcar lines) to the Queensboro Bridge line for shuttle service over the East River bridge of its name. The primary function of this New York City line was to serve Welfare Island with its hospital complex, midway on the bridge. The cars were 42′ long and rolled on 26″ wheels. The photo was taken in 1951.

Photo: Francis J. Goldsmith

THE MOTOR DRIVE

The electric streetcar "took off" early in 1888 when Frank J. Sprague's successful operation in Richmond, Virginia, was launched using 40 cars with axle-hung motors. Before that Siemens used motors mounted on rubber pads under the car floor between the axles, power being transmitted through steel cables from the armature to drums on the axles. In 1883 Siemens had electrified the 2.8 mile line between Moedling and Hinterbruehl, south of Vienna, using 1" slotted gas pipes for the overhead, with cars pulling the inside-running current collectors.

The 17' L x 6'-6" W, 5 ton cars rested on a 4'-11" wheelbase. They were powered by a 12½ hp 600 rpm motor mounted between the axles, both of which were driven by trains of spur gears. As soon as wear caused the slightest difference in wheel diameters, this caused a "most infamous noise." As pointed out years sooner by James Watt, noise means wear, so this first attempt at monomotor drive was short-lived: the layout was soon modified so the motor would drive only one axle.

Van Depoele mounted the motor in his single end car on the front platform and placed the control on top of the motor. An intermediate gear and chain drive connected motor to front axle. However, the car platform, designed from horsecar experience, could not take the motor weight and the drive load, which put an end to further development of that concept. Its principal legacy was the name "motorman" for the driver who stood out on the platform next to the machine.

With Sprague and his successors having a monopoly on the axle-hung motor idea, Siemens was stuck with the chain drive, but in their case with underfloor motor driving both axles. This solution was used as late as 1895 with the 21' 5 ton cars supplied to the Basel (Switzerland) Street Railways, powered by 15 hp 360 rpm motors. The chains ran in oil-filled casings. A primitive control switch provided four steps. Braking was effected by a counterbalanced throw-over lever.

As the axle-hung motor became more generally favored, so did opinion that it would be more effective to support the motor in line with its center-of-gravity, a solution adopted on some contracts by Ganz & Company of Budapest (Hungary). Unfortunately this increased the share of motor weight carried directly on the axle from about 29% to 64%, so the original layout proved to be the most effective one.

Another concept was offered in the Eickemeyer-Field truck, incorporating a single 20 hp motor supported by helical springs on the axles and directly driving both axles by means of a crank and connecting rods. This truck achieved a fully sprung motor but at the cost of weighing a heavy 4 tons. Single-truck cars using this design were tried (1890-1891) in Toledo, Ohio, and Yonkers, New York. Double-truckers appeared for a short while in Boston, Massachusetts, and Lynchburg, Virginia. Sadly, the side rods excited unpleasant shaking vibrations, though in Boston reference was made only to "waddling," to the design being hard on the track, and to the motors not having enough power. Lynchburg's cars had difficulty negotiating curves and derailed at the slightest provocation.

Rod drives applied to electric traction mandate close and frequent maintenance. Bearing clearances must be adjusted, for example, more precisely than steam locomotives, since there is no "free end" corresponding to the piston, and consequently the centers between all crank pins must be rigidly maintained. Any wear at these points will cause excessive stresses and bearing pressures. Conversion of the uniform motor torque into a reciprocating motion produces severe stress in motor shaft, jackshaft and framing, leading to bending and fracture of pins and rods. Such problems were the subject of extensive research in 1914 and 1924, mainly by Swiss and German scientists and engineers under the title "Schuettelschwingungen" (shaking oscillations). It prescribed tight dimensional control and bearing maintenance.

Further side rod drives were tried in Cincinnati and Pittsburgh. In these applications, one axle of each truck of a double-truck car was powered by a motor mounted in the usual axle-hung manner, while the other axle was coupled by means of a side rod at each end. Five such cars were acquired by Cincinnati in 1911, using 75 hp motors. Noise and vibration caused them to be replaced by Brill maximum traction trucks. Pittsburgh's

experience was similar. Further development along these lines occurred on the 5-mile Muelheim-Badenweiler (Germany) interurban, whose five 1000 v DC side-rod cars maintained service from 1941 to 1955. A sample was tried in Bradford (England) in 1927 as prototype for a 250-car fleet, but it remained the sole such unit there. A side-rod equipped work car, wreck car #1011 of the Key System lines of Oakland, California, remains today in operable condition at the Bay Area railway museum, Rio Vista, California.

Development of a longitudinally placed motor driving both truck axles goes back to Percy Priestly, General Manager of Liverpool Corporation Tramways, who in 1929 spent Ł2445 sterling on a 37' single-deck car with 50" wheelbase trucks each containing one 60 hp motor driving 24" wheels. Ten double-deck cars also incorporated these trucks, but Priestly's death in 1932 put an end to further development.

A light-weight single-motor truck design was evolved about the same time by Ernst Kreissig, engineering manager of the Uerdingen car works, and Walter Prasse, chief engineer of cars and shops of the Essen (Germany) street railways. It was first used in 1933 under two 41'-6" L x 85" W 11.6 ton cars. The longitudinally placed 55 hp motor formed the backbone of this truck. It had a kingpin extending up from its housing that rested via rigid arms on one axle, with the other end supported from the other axle via hinged arms and quarter-elliptic springs. This provided the 3-point suspension capable of following the twists of a track. Rubber cushioned wheels were used. The 57" wheelbase trucks incorporated bevel drive. Brake drums were used for the hand-operated parking brake, dynamic braking being used for service and emergency stops. Twenty similar, but shorter, cars, better suited for operation through narrow-center curves and powered with 80 hp motors, were added in 1938-1940.

The design was taken up and further developed by Brown Boveri, whose "Simplex" version was applied to a number of Swiss cars. Modifications were introduced later to permit fully-sprung mounting of motors, two of which were carried in the truck parallel to the axles.

It was the original Kreissig-Prasse Essen design which gave impetus after WW II to development of a number of single-motor trucks widely applied in the west. However, without going into mathematical detail relating to the forces and wear resulting from two closely-coupled wheelsets, it is certain that the slightest difference in wheel diameters will force one wheelset to slip with respect to the other, regardless of power input. Even when coasting the drive connecting the two will have to deal with the torque as limited by wheel/rail adhesion, thus increasing both wear and tractive resistance.

Furthermore, as shown in 1956 by extensive tests carried out on road vehicles, and in 1962 on a 4-wheel monomotor truck the following conclusions apply:
- With all wheel diameters exactly alike, greater friction-related work and wear will be encountered by the rear wheels when driving and by the front ones when braking,
- When driving, more work will be done by the larger wheels regardless of whether leading or trailing,
- When braking, the smaller wheels will be subject to greater wear regardless of whether leading or trailing,
- The wear of the two wheelsets will differ the more, the greater the difference of their diameters, and,
- The difference in the rate of wheel wear will increase with the tractive or braking efforts imposed.

This means that any differences in wheel diameter would tend to be reduced if the service calls mainly for motoring. On the other hand, braking at torques in excess of mean motoring levels would slow or even reverse the equalizing impact on wheel diameter difference. However, neither of these effects would eliminate the power circulation circuit or the wear which takes place between the wheelsets whether motoring, coasting or braking! Such wear and stress which itself tends to cause the paired wheels toward different diameters can only be minimized by maintaining wheel diameters as nearly equal as possible. Present good practice calls for the difference between wheelsets paired to a motor not to exceed 0.08".

83

Most recent monomotor truck designs are based on the longitudinally placed machine driving both axles via flexible couplings, thus providing resilient suspension without relying on the truck proper. The latter is supported by axleboxes via rubber springs, while the car body is carried by helical or air springs.

A new development of some promise is the use of two squirrel-cage rotors placed within a single longitudinal motor shell. Each rotor drives the adjoining axle. Experience with existing monomotor drives has not been overlooked by the leading electrical manufacturers. One of them states that the new concept will be "of advantage, compared with the monomotor, since the wheelsets are mechanically uncoupled, the individual axle drive permitting greater diameter differences of the truck wheelsets."

Another supplier points out that "a certain disadvantage of the (monomotor) arrangement is that both truck axles are rigidly connected by the motor. This can cause wheel and rail wear. . . . The use of three-phase motors will permit the use of two counter-rotating rotors coupled solely by the rotating electric field, permitting a certain degree of speed difference. Thus, both axles will be elastically coupled without forsaking the advantages of individual axle drives."

At last the drawbacks inherent in the recent practice of driving two axles by a common motor are starting to be appreciated. A long overdue return to some kind of individual drive may be imminent. Certainly this should improve maintenance and reduce energy costs. The challenge will be to keep the complication, space and weight of power-conditioning packages for the electrical equipment from cancelling out the benefits concerned.

J. L. K.

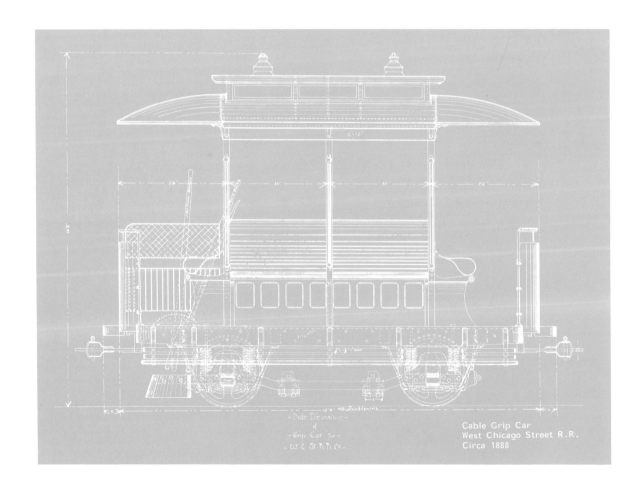

Cable Grip Car
West Chicago Street R.R.
Circa 1888

84

United Traction Company 301

An especially unusual car was developed by a cooperative effort between United Traction (the local street railway of Albany, New York), the Cincinnati Car Corporation and the General Electric Company. Completed late in 1929, its carbody, 42'-8½" long, was largely aluminum. It was mounted on Cincinnati arch bar trucks and powered with four GE-265 motors rated 35 hp. With 26" wheels and line voltage of 550 v DC, this provided a free speed of 32 mph with acceleration of 3.5 mphps. Control was foot-operated, GE type PCM. Braking, also foot-controlled, was self-lapping straight air, supplemented by magnetic track brakes. This photo of the distinctive sample car was taken in 1942.

Photo: Lawson K. Hill

D.C. Transit System, 1053

▲ The trend to a different car design that began about 1928 accelerated in 1935. There was hope that a better vehicle might help transit hold more of its sagging ridership. Washington's Capital Traction Company in 1935 ordered 10 cars each from Brill and St. Louis Car to incorporate the latest ideas in streamlining and technology. Here we see #1053, one of the St. Louis group, as it looked in 1948. Both the Brill and St. Louis cars were about 44 ft. long and weighed 35,000 lbs. The St. Louis cars had General Electric propulsion packages, with type 1193, 50 hp motors and 22-notch control, and they had the first production line all-welded bodies built for street railway service. Resilient wheels were used on some. Custom trucks were designated "Capital 70." Maximum acceleration of 4.75 mphps and braking up to 8 mphps were claimed.

Des Moines Railway 708

▲◀ In the middle of 1930 the Cummings Car & Coach Company of Paris, Illinois delivered 50 lightweight, single-end city cars of an advanced design to the Des Moines (Iowa) Railway. Having a rather interurban-ish style, these cars were 42 ft. long, weighed 35,300 lbs., and rode on Cummings 64 MCB type trucks with 26" wheels. The General Electric power package included four GE-247, 40 hp motors and K-75 control, with which these cars could accelerate at a respectable 3 mphps and run at a free speed close to 40 mph. In 1940 Des Moines had about 130 cars running over 73 track miles. Photo taken 1948; streetcar service ended in 1951.

Atlantic City Transportation Company 202

◀◀ Brill's answer to the challenge of the middle 1930s for a better car was not to join in the common effort known as the President's Conference Committee (which developed the PCC car) but to produce its own design, carrying on from the work it had done on a sample car for Chicago Surface Lines and the lot of ten for Capital Transit. While the "Brilliner" was an attractive vehicle, even incorporating some styling ideas of the noted Raymond Loewy, Brill's independent approach cost it industry support and marked a turning point from this company's predominant position as a streetcar builder. Photo taken along the ocean shore in 1953.

Three photos: Eugene Van Dusen

Los Angeles Metropolitan Transit Authority 3001

▲ This car was introduced to the public on March 23, 1937 by Los Angeles' Mayor Shaw, LARy President Storrs and child movie star Shirley Temple. PCC's had come to stay for the quarter century until abandonment of street-cars in 1963. Car #3001, shown here in 1959, was one of a first lot which included 60 cars. Their performance represented substantial improvement over the best cars then in service; a 60% increase in acceleration, 90% in braking and 40% in maximum speed. With an overall length of 46 ft., they rode on Clark B-2 trucks for 42" gage track. They had 25" wheels. Westinghouse control and four W-1432 (55 hp) motors. All 165 PCC's of this city were built by St. Louis Car. At this writing, car #3001 is preserved at the Orange Empire Railway Museum in Perris, California.

Photo: Eugene Van Dusen

San Francisco Municipal Railway 1002

▲ ◄ San Francisco cautiously approached the new PCC concept with an order of five, locally dubbed "Magic Carpet Cars," that were brought into service late in 1939. Their unusual double-end end-door-only layout (plus the fact that two of the five cars ordered were placed on Brill's 97-ER-1 trucks unauthorized by Transit Research Corporation, holder of the PCC patents) led to a squabble over license fees and designation as PCC's. Unique on this lot was the use of hand instead of foot-operated master controllers, called "Cinestons." Ten similar double-end PCC cars were added in 1948, followed by conventional floor-plan cars (the last built in the U.S.A.) in 1951-1952. They were 50'-5" long. Car #1001 had General Electric propulsion. This photo: 1949.

Photo: Henry Stange, Jr.

Brooklyn & Queens Transit Corporation 1094

◄◄ The Brooklyn system was active in the development of the PCC, even providing a proving ground for early hardware tests. It was the first property to place a firm order for PCC's and deliveries of its initial production run of 99-46 ft. cars (#1001-1099) were made by St. Louis Car Company between October 1936 and January 1937. This photo was made in 1949.

Photo: Thomas A. Lesh

89

Pacific Electric Railway 5000

For its heavily-loaded urban/suburban Glendale-Burbank and (for a couple of years) the Venice Short Line route, Pacific Electric in 1940 ordered thirty PCC's from Pullman-Standard Car Mfg. Co. P-S assigned all PCC jobs to its Worcester, Massachusetts plant. With a length of 53'-10" over pulling faces, PE#3000-3029 were the longest PCC's ever built. The seating was also unusual for a PCC, with reversible cross-seats and fold-down seats over the step wells giving a total seating of 59. This air/electric car complete weighed 41,600 lbs. and when delivered was set to acceleration and braking rates of 4.5 mphps. Top free speed was about 42 mph.

They were also unusual in having double-end Peter Witt type floor plan and they were the first PCC's to have provision for train operation with Westinghouse couplers and multiple-unit control. In later years the cars were operated one-man and door control was modified to permit the center left door to be controlled from the operator's dash. This photo, taken at the west terminal, Orange Grove at Glenoaks, dates to 1953; PCC service by PE in the Los Angeles area ended in 1955 and the cars moved overseas to end their days serving commuters in Buenos Aires.

Photo: R. L. Day

Toronto Transportation Commission 4161

    An enthusiastic user of PCC equipment, Toronto started its fleet with an order of 140 cars in 1938 and kept adding both new and second-owner cars until its fleet totalled 745. Operating on 58⅞" track gage, all were approximately 46 ' long, 8'-3⅜" wide cars ranging from 35,000 -37,000 lb. weight. They had Westinghouse electrical equipment and B-2 trucks and were single-end front-entrance-center exit. Many were equipped for two-car train operation. Several of the minor varieties within the fleet were captured together in this scene at Lansdowne barn on Toronto's west side in 1948.

Photo: Robert V. Mehlenbeck

Montreal Transportation Commission 3502

Although its streetcar fleet numbered nearly a thousand cars and at one time was one of North America's most innovative, having originated the Pay-As-You-Enter car, Montreal's interest in PCC's apparently was too little and came too late. A lot of only 18 cars, #3500-3517, was delivered by Canadian Car & Foundry Company in March 1944, using car shells supplied by St. Louis Car. It was wartime and that was all they could get. They were the 46 ft. air/electric standard pre-war model with B-2 trucks and Westinghouse electrical package. Use of a dash illuminator cowl instead of a headlight is noted. This photo of #3502 dates to 1959. Service by streetcar ended in Montreal that same year. Only car #3517 was saved, going to the museum line at Delson, Quebec.

Photo: George Krambles

Baltimore Transit Company 7142

Baltimore was a property that "came early and bought often" as far as PCC's were concerned, with seven orders in the period 1936-1943 totalling 275 cars, split between St. Louis Car and Pullman-Standard, and between General Electric and Westinghouse. In the 1955 photo presented here, GE cars representing the 1941 and 1943 orders are shown in the storage yard at Gardenville, in northeast Baltimore. The property was unique in having 64½″ track gage. Streetcar service died in 1963, but one PCC has been preserved and restored at the Baltimore Streetcar Museum, similarly unique for its track gage.

Photo: George Krambles

93

Louisville Railway 502

A number of transit systems seriously considered application of PCC cars. Pittsburgh Railways cooperated by loaning a car for test in interested cities. Louisville, Kentucky was one of these. It holds the questionable honor of ▲ being the place that came closest to using PCC's, with an order of 25 of the 46 ft. all-electric model. A report submitted by public utility consultant John H. Bickley in 1940 recommended bus conversion of all routes except Fourth Street, which exceeded all others in gross receipts, car miles and passengers carried. Bickley stated "The most feasible course in the betterment of Fourth Street is the installation of 20 PCC . . . cars." Unfortunately, World War II's hiatus delayed the actual order until 1945. By 1946, when 15 of the 25 cars (including #502 shown here) had been delivered, the postwar surge in automobile registrations coupled with the track/plant rehab needed after wartime deferred maintenance caused a change of heart. Louisville traded its PCC's to Cleveland for buses and cash. Except for the Pittsburgh test car, no PCC's actually ran in regular service in Louisville. In 1953 the 56½" gage Cleveland system sold their ex-Louisville 60" gage cars to the 58½" Toronto lines, where as #4675-4699 they ran on until 1983. Got that?

Photo: Dr. Howard Blackburn

Cincinnati Street Railway 1000

Cincinnati, Ohio began its evaluation of modern high-performance streetcar designs with 1939 orders of one each of St. Louis Car PCC, Pullman-Standard PCC, and Brilliner. The Pullman sample, #1000, shown here when nearly ► ▲ new, was the basic 46' air/electric model. Later renumbered #1127, it remained on the Cincinnati property until 1951 while the production run of 52 St. Louis Car PCC's was sold to Toronto in 1950. Cincinnati's street railway used 62½" track gage and double-trolley power distribution.

Photo: Frank E. Butts

St. Louis Public Service Company 1530

St. Louis, Missouri was an extensive user of PCC's, amassing some 300 in three lots delivered 1940, 1941 and 1946, all from the local St. Louis Car Company. The basic 46' model was adopted, using 58" gage B-2 trucks, but ► ► the electrical equipment for each lot was divided between General Electric and Westinghouse. SLPS President over much of the PCC acquisition period was W.T. Rossell, who, before coming to St. Louis, had been associated with development of the PCC, particularly the all-electric version.

Beginning in 1954, St. Louis' began to phase out streetcars until by 1966 all were gone. PCC's were sold off to many buyers including Philadelphia, San Francisco, Shaker Heights and Tampico (Mexico). Shown in this 1950 scene is #1530, one of the first order for St. Louis.

Photo: Eugene Van Dusen

96

Kansas City Public Service Company 529

▲   Kansas City, Missouri began to use PCC's in 1940, with an order of 24 air/electric cars from St. Louis Car. A further 160 PCC's were acquired in 1946-1947, this time the post-war all-electric type but with higher side windows instead of standee windows. Shown above is #529 of that type. Streetcar service ended in Kansas City in 1957 and the postwar cars were sold off, some to Tampico, some to Toronto and the equipment from others to Belgium.

Photo: Eugene Van Dusen

Metropolitan Transit Authority 3324

▲ ◄   The Boston system went through a number of name changes. In 1958 as MTA it acquired 25 unusual PCC's from the Dallas (Texas) Transit System where they had run from 1945 to 1956. They had been built by Pullman-Standard, with an overall length of 47', Westinghouse air/electric equipment and B-2 trucks. The double-end, end-door floor plan which had been chosen to permit operation on routes whose terminals had crossovers, not loops, proved suitable for some applications in Boston and not objectionable for others. In this 1959 scene, #3324 is shown meeting an interesting old Mack motorbus.

Photo: Norton D. Clark

Chicago Surface Lines 7109

◄ ◄   With 683 PCC streetcars in its fleet, Chicago set the American record for PCC car buys from original builders while Toronto took honors as operator of the largest fleet of PCC's with 745, including its second-owner units. Chicago's cars were unusual in using rear entrance and in large size, being 50' long by 108" wide. Its postwar orders had been delayed by procurement and funding problems. In the meantime auto registrations were skyrocketing and rail operation/maintenance in street traffic became intolerable. CTA began the change to buses at once. Ultimately 570 of the 600 cars ordered postwar were salvaged, with motors, control, seats, lights, etc., all being reused in PCC rapid transit cars, many of which remain in service at this writing.

  In this 1949 scene, all-electric St. Louis-built streetcar #7109 prepares to cross Roosevelt Road southbound from the Loop area on Clark Street.

Photo: Eugene Van Dusen   97

Shaker Heights Rapid Transit 71

The Department of Transportation of the City of Shaker Heights, Ohio, operated transit service connecting the east side suburbs to Terminal Tower in the heart of Cleveland. Originally operated with center-door cars (shown elsewhere in this volume), the fleet was modernized and enhanced in 1947 with the purchase of 25 PCC's from Pullman-Standard. These cars had 50' long, 9' wide bodies, single-end front-entrance-center-exit but (as in comparable Boston cars) a double-stream center door was also provided on the left side to accomodate loading needs in the Union Terminal. The cars had General Electric all-electric equipment for multiple-unit operation and trains of up to six cars were scheduled. Later Shaker (and later its current owner, greater Cleveland Regional Transit Authority) acquired second-owner units from Minneapolis, St. Louis, Newark and Toronto and even borrowed two ex-Illinois Terminal cars from museums while awaiting long delayed new generation light rail cars from Italy. This photo was taken in 1950.

Photo: Charles A. Brown

Port Authority of Allegheny County 1754

Best known today as PATransit, the Pittsburgh system had at its peak 666 PCC's, making it a close second to Chicago as a new PCC buyer. Pittsburgh's #100, in March 1936, became the first PCC in the world. It was a 46′ air/electric car, riding on B-2 trucks. It was followed by more orders, all from St. Louis Car, until there were 565 similar ones in the fleet. Postwar, Pittsburgh got the prototype all-electric and followed it with a run of 99 more. This group had sealed windows and a high velocity air circulating system that traded off arm-out-of-window accidents against some noise and temperature discomfort for riders. One of these, #1754, is shown in this 1966 view at E. Pittsburgh. Many of this type car remain in regular services at this writing.

Photo: Anthony J. Schill

99

D.C. Transit System 1512

▲ Washington, the nation's capital, ordered its first 45 PCC cars in 1937 and was well enough pleased to keep adding to the fleet until by 1944 it had 489 of them. At approximately 44' overall, they were a little shorter than typical. They were all built by St. Louis Car and rode on B-2 trucks. An unusual requirement was the capability to operate from underground conduit or alternatively, from the usual trolley. Car #1512, shown here in 1958, was overhauled and improved in 1957, adding air-conditioning and flourescent lighting. It remained a popular car in regular and charter service until streetcar service ended in Washington in 1962. Although donation to the National Capital Historical Museum of Transportation in 1970 was intended to assure its preservation, it was destroyed by vandals a year later.

Photo: LeRoy O. King, Jr.

Philadelphia Transportation Company 2799

▲◄ Another extensive user of PCC cars has been Philadelphia, both in the city system and the suburban Red Arrow division, which between them have peaked at about 500 such vehicles. They have ranged from 1948-model air/electric cars, through postwar all-electrics (of which #2799 shown here in 1947 was one) and second-hand St. Louis, Kansas City and Toronto cars. South Eastern Pennsylvania Transportation Authority (SEPTA), which took over the area's transit services, has replaced much of the older equipment with new generation light rail vehicles.

Photo: Thomas H. Desnoyers

Illinois Terminal Railroad System 457

◄◄ One of the smaller PCC applications was on the suburban service between St. Louis, Missouri and Granite City, Illinois. Because of the barrier of the Mississippi River between the two communities, a modest volume of commuter traffic between them had developed on the Illinois Terminal, an electric railroad originally designed to be an interurban link between St. Louis and various Illinois cities such as Peoria, Springfield, Champaign, etc. In 1949 ITRR received eight PCC cars of a special double-end design, 50'-5" long x 9' wide, with General Electric multiple-unit control. They were operated with two-man crews, the conductor stationed just behind the motorman as in Mitten's "Nearside" cars of nearly four decades earlier. Shown here in Granite City in 1952.

Photo: William C. Janssen

JURY LEONID KOFFMAN

With Bulletin 125, CERA proudly introduces an old friend and new contributor to our knowledge of the history and technology of electric railways, Jury Leonid Koffman, Mechanical and Electrical Engineer. He is responsible for the several sidebar stories which supplement the color plates and their captions. His unusual background is in itself a story of the development of the industry and the hobby of its study.

Jury Koffman was born in 1911 in Dnepropetrovsk, in the southern Ukraine on the Dneiper River within about 150 miles of the Black Sea. His grandfather started as a coal miner, became a foreman and ran ships on the Volga to Iran, making, Jury notes, 100% profit each way. He became a banker at Dnepropetrovsk involved with real estate, mines, and steel works, but died in 1934 employed as a night watchman.

Jury's father studied law and owned a steel mill at Dnepropetrovsk, steel works at nearby Kharkov, and a film studio at Odessa. He was killed near the latter city in 1919 at only 37 years of age by bandits. Mother kept the family going by selling jewelry and giving language lessons.

After shutting down during World War I Dnepropetrovsk trams started running again in 1923. Young Jury spent his free time with the two men who coupled and uncoupled trailers left behind by cars going up a 10% grade. This gave him the opportunity to become friends with most crews. He was also "allowed" to couple and uncouple cars and to test the brakes. There had been originally two tram companies, but now the Belgian one with two lines had been combined into the other, a municipal operation also with two lines. At age 15 he went to one of the depots and got to know Alexander Ivanovich Kirstein, a German who came with some German-built cars and stayed on to be rolling stock superintendent. Since Jury already could speak German, he became friends with Kirstein and at age 15½, became an apprentice (and, of course, drove trams). By 18 (coming of age in Russia) he was a regular driver and then became assistant to Kirstein.

By 1932 Koffman was in Danzig on the Baltic Sea working on inspection and construction of trawlers and tugs built for Russia by F. Schichau & Co. He then took an opportunity to work for the same company at its works in Elbing, East Prussia, where he became familiar with building steam locomotives.

In those depression days there was much unemployment and Russian orders were very welcome. Next, Koffman studied electrical engineering at the Berlin Technical University and worked at the traction design office of AEG (German General Electric Company), where again, Russian orders were working wonders. Diploma work for Jury included design of a high speed Co-Co locomotive, overhead and substation layout under Privy Councilor, Dr. Eng., Dr. Eng, h.c. Walter Reichel, Professor of Electric Railway Engineering at the Technical University of Berlin, inventor of the bow collector and engineer of the famous Marienfeld-Zossen high speed tests of 1903. For a short while, he worked with Deutsche Getriebe Company, makers of mechanical transmissions for railcars and locos, and designers/consultants for complete vehicles. It was there he met Dorothea, his future wife, who was then a school girl. She later studied medicine at Prague, continuing after WW II at Bern and Geneva, to reach qualification in Bern.

In November 1936 Jury was arrested by the Gestapo on suspicion of anti-Hitler activities and was held in solitary in their headquarters. But that's another story, not part of traction background except for encouraging Koffman to go elsewhere. It was winter; Jury had no Polish transit visa, but he meant to go to England and had a two-week permit to study there. So they put him on a boat in Hamburg headed for Southampton, where he arrived in January 1937.

There Brian Reed of *Railway Gazette* and A. R. Bell of *The Locomotive*, for whom Koffman had written from time to time, helped him with a room near Holborn, while Mylius of Deutsche Getriebe sent him £2 a week to see what the market possibilities were like. This brought him in touch with D. Wickham & Company, who offered him the post of railcar designer. Since he liked the country, risked imprisonment in Germany and was in no hurry to return to Russia, he joined them to design some very light and novel diesel railcars for the Central Railway of Peru, the Kenya & Uganda Railway and the Jamaica Government Railways, All had positively guided axles (no horn guides, just arms) and flexicoil suspension, this in 1938 being Koffman's first substantial original action.

In 1942 he was asked to join the Department of Tank Design of the Ministry of Supply as Assistant Engineer 1 in charge of design, development and testing of cooling systems for army vehicles, tanks, etc. This was because of some papers he had written on cooling and on propeller railcars. Promoted to Principal Scientific Officer and Engineer 1, he took over development of novel prime movers.

In 1946 he became a British citizen. In 1956 he moved to Derby to take on the post of Assistant Superintendent, Vehicle and Track Division, British Rail Research Department and later back to London to join the Chief Mechanical Engineer, BR, as Mechanical Engineer (Projects). This dealt with design of all new running gear which in 1958 was a predominant problem. He became Mechanical and Electrical Engineer (Development) to deal with cars, freight stock, diesel and electric locomotives. He retired from this in 1972 but went on to become a consultant for Hong Kong's Mass Transit Railway, Amtrak, Via Canada, Australian Mining Railways, Dunlop Company, and others.

His writings in the trade press are extensive, as are his contributions to German periodicals such as *Der Stadtverkehr*, *Strassenbahn Magazin*, and *Lok Magazin*. He was contributing technical information to *Electric Traction* magazine in 1930, eight years before CERA was formed.

In the reminiscences of E. S. Cox, Assistant Chief Mechanical and Electrical Engineer of British Rail, Cox states, "We had the advantage of the wide theoretical and practical experience of Jury Koffman, well known throughout the world for his contributions to the literature of vehicle riding. First as a member of the Research Department, but later working with us directly, he was able to check, and where necessary, modify every bogie design which was offered for the first 174 and subsequent diesel locomotives, as well as for the AC electric locomotives. Riding problems of any consequence were either completely absent or quickly solved, and harmful effects on the tracks have simply not appeared at all, to the considerable relief of the civil engineers, and to the relief of all the mechanical engineers."

Also, quoting the history of the Institute of Locomotive Engineers, "The quality of vehicle riding in this country has been improved out of all recognition by the work of Koffman and his associates, who, combining the results of research abroad with their own native experimental development work, have, in seven papers since 1948, placed the subject upon altogether new footing."

The CERA publication team is delighted to have this distinguished colleague returning, as he puts it, "to my first love, street railways."

G.K.

TABLE OF CONTENTS

BIBLIOGRAPHY

The broad general base of reference for the captions and descriptions as well as the essays contained in this book are the publications of the trade press of the electric railway industry for the period from the 1880s to the present. Another, and equally valuable source, was the collective observations and records of individual historians and enthusiasts who are generally included in the acknowledgments at the beginning of this book. The most significant of these are listed below.

For brevity, in the case of those many references drawn from parts of a continuing series of publications from a single source, only that source is referenced and not the individual issues used.

Listings are alphabetical by author, except where no author was identified the listing is by title.

Baker, John E.
    WINNIPEG'S ELECTRIC TRANSIT
    Railfare Enterprises Ltd., 1982
Bickley, John E.
    REPORT, THE LOUISVILLE RAILWAY
    published by author, 1940
Binns, Richard M.
    MONTREAL'S ELECTRIC STREET CARS
    Railfare Enterprises Ltd., 1973
Blake (Henry W.) and Jackson (Walter)
    ELECTRIC RAILWAY TRANSPORTATION
    McGraw-Hill, 1915
Boorse, J. W., Jr.

PHILADELPHIA IN MOTION
    Bryn Mawr Press, 1976
BRILL MAGAZINE, and Brill Catalogs
    J. G. Brill Co., 1906-1938
Bromley (John F.) and May (Jack)
    FIFTY YEARS OF PROGRESSIVE TRANSIT
    Electric Railroaders' Association, 1973
Central Electric Railfans' Association
    Bulletins 1 - 123, 1938 to date
CHICAGO & WEST TOWNS RAILWAY
    Electric Railway Historical Society
    Ca 1950
Corley, Raymond F.
    PCC CARS IN THE U.S. & CANADA
    Compilation of collected notes, 1948 et. seq.
Cox, Dr. Harold E.
    PCC CARS IN NORTH AMERICA
    published by author, 1963
Cummings (Luther P.) and Rohrbeck (Benson W.)
    GARDEN SPOT TROLLEYS
    Ben Rohrbeck Traction Publications, 1977
Dodge, R. V.
    RAILS OF THE SILVER GATE
    Pacific Railway Journal, 1960
Farrell, Michael M.
    WHO MADE ALL OUR STREETCARS GO?
    Baltimore NRHS Publications, 1973
Fetters (Thomas) and Swanson (Peter W., Jr.)
    PIEDMONT & NORTHERN RAILWAY
    Golden West Books, 1974
Fetters, Thomas
    PALMETTO TRACTION
    published by Harold E. Cox, 1978
Foesig, Harry
    TROLLEYS OF BERKS COUNTY, PA
    published by Harold E. Cox, 1971
GENERAL ELECTRIC COMPANY
    various Bulletins and Publications
HEADLIGHTS
    Electric Railroaders' Association, 1950 - date
Hennick (Louis C.) and Charlton (E. Harper)
    THE STREETCARS OF NEW ORLEANS
    Pelican Publishing Co., 1975
Keenan, Jack
    CINCINNATI & LAKE ERIE R.R.
    Golden West Books, 1974
King, LeRoy O., Jr.
    100 YEARS OF CAPITAL TRACTION
    Taylor Publishing Company, 1972
Lind, Alan R.
    FROM HORSECARS TO STREAMLINERS
    Transport History Press, 1978
MASS TRANSPORTATION
MASS TRANSPORTATION DIRECTORY
ELECTRIC TRACTION
    Kenfield-Davis Publishing Co., 1910-1945
McGRAW ELECTRIC RAILWAY DIRECTORY

McGRAW ELECTRIC RAILWAY MANUAL
McGraw-Hill Publishing Co., 1899-1914
POOR'S MANUAL of AMERICAN STREET RYS.
Poor's Railroad Manual, 1893
Pursley, Louis H.
THE TORONTO TROLLEY CAR STORY
Interurbans, 1961
Rohrbeck, Benson W.
PENNSYLVANIA'S STREET RAILWAYS
Ben Rohrbeck Traction Publications, 1982
Schneider (Fred W. III) and Carlson (Stephen P.)
PCC FROM COAST TO COAST
Interurbans Press, 1983
PCC, THE CAR THAT FOUGHT BACK
Interurbans Press, 1980
Smallwood, Charles
THE WHITE FRONT CARS OF
SAN FRANCISCO
Interurbans Press, 1978
Swett, Ira L.
CARS OF PACIFIC ELECTRIC
Interurbans, 1964
Swett, Ira L.
CARS OF THE SACRAMENTO NORTHERN
Interurbans, 1963
Swett, Ira L.
LINES OF THE PACIFIC ELECTRIC—
West Dist.
Interurbans, 1957
TRANSIT JOURNAL
ELECTRIC RAILWAY JOURNAL
STREET RAILWAY JOURNAL
McGraw-Hill Publishing Co., 1899-1942
Wagner (Richard M. and Birdella)
CURVED SIDE CARS
Wagner Publishing, 1965
Wagner (Richard M.) and Wright (Roy J.)
CINCINNATI STREETCARS #7, #9
Trolley Talk, 1976, 1984
Walker, Jim
KEY SYSTEM ALBUM
Interurbans Press, 1978
Walker, Jim
THE YELLOW CARS OF LOS ANGELES
Interurbans Press, 1977
Wonson (Richard L.) and Frazier (Paul W.)
THE RHODE ISLAND CO., Part I
The Branford Elec. Ry. Assoc., Ca 1968
WESTINGHOUSE ELECTRIC & MFG. CO.
Bulletins and Publications, 1907-1945

INDEX A — Personalities

Hill, Lawson K., 5, 26, 85
Hitler, A., 102
Hopkinson, Dr. E., 37
Huntington, H. E., 28

Jackson, W., 27
Janssen, Wm. C., 4, 5, 40, 101
Johnson, Tom L., 31
Jones, P. N., 46

Kashin, Seymour, 5
Keevil, W. R., 4
Kerchum, R. T., 5
Kerr, A. D., 5
King, LeRoy O., Jr., 5, 54, 101
Kirstein, A. I., 102
Kocan, Peter, 5
Koffman, Dorothea, 102
Koffman, J. L., (J.L.K.), 4, 5, 15, 28, 32, 38, 56, 75, 76, 84, 102
Krambles, G. K., (G.K.), 4, 5, 92, 93, 102
Kreissig, Ernst, 83

Lenin, V. I., 15
Lesh, Thomas A., 5, 39, 89
Lloyd, Gordon E., 5, 46
Lloyd, Morris H., 5
Loewy, Raymond, 87
Lonnes, Fred D., 4
Lucas, John H., 53
Lukin, Richard N., 5

MacCorquodale, D. C., 4
Magee, Louis, 76
McCaleb, W. A., 5
McClelland, Gen. G., 50
McDonald, Duncan, 27
McKinley, G. G., 5, 21, 60, 67
Mehlenbeck, R. V., 5, 91
Middleton, W. D., 5
Mitten, T. E., 27, 28, 29, 32, 34, 36, 55, 101
Moffat, Bruce, 4
Mylius, O., 102

Neddin, W. F., 5
Nettis, S. A., 4

O'Shaughnessy, M. M., 8
Ost, Paul J., 8

Parshall, —, 11, 37
Peterson, A. H., 4, 5
Peterson, E. L., 5
Petzold, Charley W., 4
Plazzotta, R. A., 4
Pommer, Eugene, 76
Potter, W. B., 11, 37
Prasse, Walter, 83

Priestly, Percy, 83
Pruden, Jerry D., 5

Rehor, John A., 5
Reichel, Prof. W., 76, 102
Ridolph, E., 5
Robertson, John H., 20
Robertson, William E., 5, 34
Ross, W. J., 27
Rossell, W. T., 94

Schill, A. J., 5, 101
Schneider, F. W., III, 5
Schriber, W. H., 5, 46
Scullin, Terence, 32
Senter, R. T., 29
Shaw, Mayor, 89
Shuman, J. P., 5, 58, 73
Smallwood, C. A., 5, 21
Smith, R., 5
Sprague, F. J., 11, 14, 27, 30, 37, 76, 83
Spreckels, J. D., 28
Stange, Henry, 5, 89
Stitzel, Art, 5, 33
Storrs, L. S., 89
Styffe, A. W., 5

Temple, Shirley, 89
Thomson, Prof. Elihu, 11, 37

Van de Poele, Karel (Van Depoele, Chas.), 76, 83
Van Dusen, Eugene, 5, 34, 36, 40, 45, 46, 49, 52, 61, 70, 78, 79, 89, 94, 97
Van Sweringen, M. J. and O. P., 21

Watt, James, 83
Whitney, —, 28
Witt, Peter, 28, 31, 33, 56, 77

Yater, George H., 5
Yerkes, Charles T., 30

INDEX B — Locations: Cities, states, provinces, countries, lakes, rivers, etc. Post Office standard abbreviations are used to designate states in which U.S.A. places are located.

Alabama (AL), 32
Albany, NY, 85
Alberta, Canada, 7, 8
Allentown, PA, 52
Altoona, PA, 81
Ansonia, CT, 76
Argentina, 56, 90
Arizona (AZ), 78
Arnhem, Holland, 56
Atlanta, GA, 7
Atlantic City, NJ, 87
Australia, 56
Austria, 31, 83

INDEX C — Companies, Publications, Schools

110

INDEX D — General

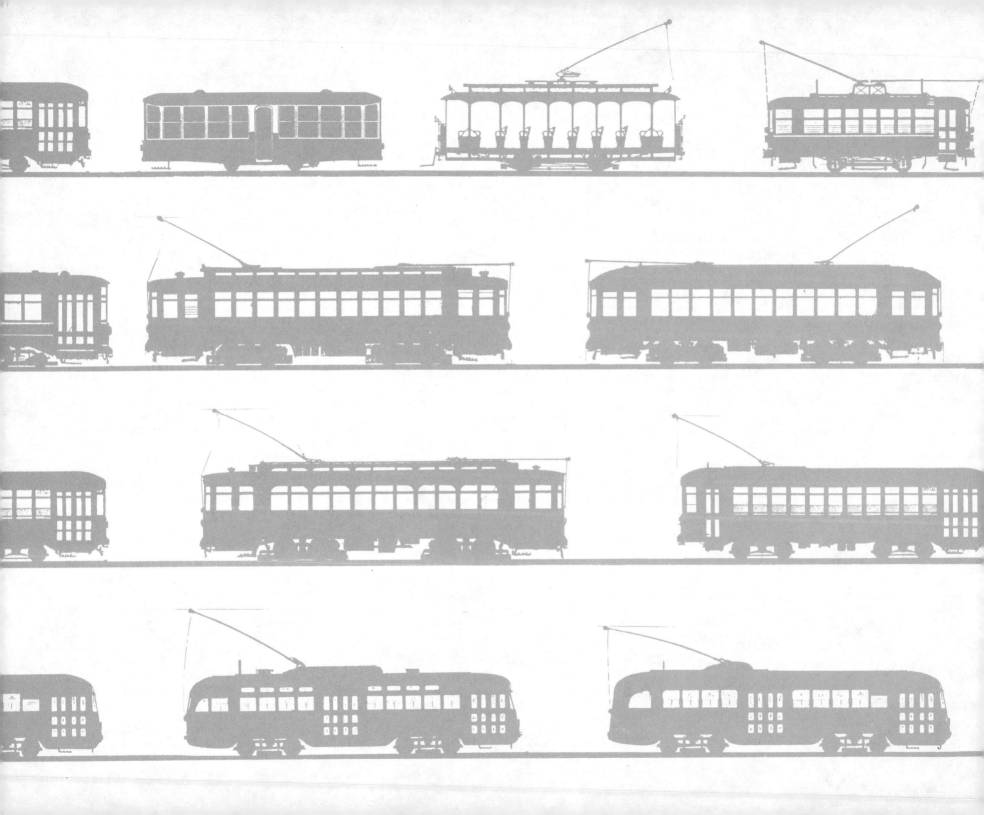